INCLUDING CHILDREN 3–11 WITH PHYSICAL DISABILITIES

Practical Guidance for Mainstream Schools

Mark

David Fulton Publishers
London

This book is dedicated to my mother, Meriel Fox, who has been much in my mind when writing this book.

David Fulton Publishers Ltd
The Chiswick Centre, 414 Chiswick High Road, London W4 5TF

www.fultonpublishers.co.uk

David Fulton Publishers is a division of Granada Learning Limited, part of the Granada Media group.

Copyright © Mark Fox 2003
10 9 8 7 6 5 4 3 2 1

British Library Cataloguing in Publication Data
A catalogue record for this book is available from the British Library.

ISBN 1–85346–937–8

Typeset by Mark Heslington, Scarborough, North Yorkshire
Printed and bound in Scotland by Scotprint, Haddington

Contents

Acknowledgements

The author wishes to thank:

The multidisciplinary Advisory Assessment Service at SCOPE;
all the children, parents and professionals who have contributed to, and lived
out, the ideas contained in this book.

Preface

This book is about the inclusion of children with physical disabilities. Inclusion means different things to different teachers. In this book it is used to denote a child with physical disabilities being included in his local mainstream or normal school. Inclusion aims to give the child as normal an education as possible. However, this is not to deny the uniqueness of the child. Children with physical difficulties may require modifications to their school, their classroom or their teaching.

A number of common features have been identified in schools where there is successful inclusion (Giangreco 1997). These features will be addressed throughout this book as the basis for effective inclusion. They are as follows:

- a shared framework
- teacher ownership
- family involvement
- clear role relationship among professionals
- collaborative teamwork
- effective use of support staff
- meaningful Statements and IEPs (Individual Educational Plans)
- procedures for evaluating effectiveness.

In addition, two other features are highlighted:

- establishing good communication
- the development of friendships.

Recent government initiatives, in particular the revised Code of Practice (DfES 2001a) and the Special Educational Needs and Disability Act (SENDA) (DfES 2001b) have promoted the inclusion of all children with Special Educational Needs (SEN) into mainstream education. However, at the moment, in Britain, though some children with a physical disability are included, many are not. The explicit purpose of this book is to help ensure that more children with physical disability are included in the mainstream. This, however, will only happen when teachers, parents, other professionals and, of course, the pupils themselves feel happy and see the benefit of inclusion. Only then will inclusion really happen for many pupils with a physical disability.

Throughout this book teachers and other professionals are referred to in the feminine, and the pupil with a physical disability in the masculine.

The different uses of the terms physical disability and physical difficulties are elaborated upon in Chapter 2. Throughout this work the terms 'the child with a physical disability' and 'the child with physical difficulties' are used interchangeably.

CHAPTER 1

Teachers' Expectations

A shared historical framework

This chapter focuses on developing a shared framework for the inclusion of children with physical disabilities. This framework is made up of the beliefs, attitudes and values of teachers, teaching assistants (TAs) and other staff in schools. These attitudes or beliefs about inclusion are important as they underpin teachers' professional practice. If practice is to change so that more children with physical disabilities are included then attitudes and beliefs also have to change. Beliefs are based on teachers' own personal experiences, but also on how others, particularly significant others, talk about inclusion. So the beliefs about the inclusion of children with physical disabilities are shaped not only by teachers' own personal experiences but also by how others in the school (for example the head teacher, the SENCO and other influential staff) talk about the issues. These beliefs and attitudes are shaped by the culture of the school. The school's culture develops over time within society's general culture. Present beliefs about inclusion are set within an historical context.

The development of special schools for children with a physical disability

Over the last 50 years there has been a radical change in the education of children with physical disabilities. This shift has been accompanied by changes in language as new views are expressed on how best these children can be educated.

After the Second World War children with disabilities were known as 'handicapped'. The 1944 Education Act defined 11 categories of handicapped pupils – including children with a physical handicap. Local education authorities (LEAs) had a responsibility to ascertain which children required special educational 'treatment'. In the 1950s and 1960s numerous special schools were set up to meet the needs of these handicapped children. Organisations such as the Spastics Society (now Scope) saw the provision of special schools as one of their prime goals. The number of special schools increased from 528 in 1945 to 743 in 1955 – with 105 of these designated for children with a physical handicap (Male 1998). By 1977 there were 1,653 special schools in England and Wales (Booth 1981). Teachers and parents were told that the placement of children with physical disabilities in special schools would ensure their best education.

The first significant change for children with physical disabilities was in 1970. Many children with severe physical disabilities and no speech had been considered ineducable. The Education Act (Handicapped Children) recognised that the 32,750 children who had previously been considered 'ineducable' were now the responsibility of LEAs. These children were almost all placed in what were known as ESN (S) schools – Educationally Subnormal (Severe) schools.

The development of integration

During the 1970s there was some questioning whether the placement of handicapped children in special schools solved their educational difficulties. This view, that children should be integrated wherever possible, was enshrined in the Warnock Report (1978) and the 1981 Education Act. Integration had a variety of meanings, but was broadly used to describe the needs of some handicapped children to be allowed to attend a normal, ordinary, or what will be referred to as a mainstream, school. The main means of integration was seen as special units attached to mainstream schools (Deno 1970). From these units children with physical disabilities could be integrated in a variety of ways:

- locational integration: the children were on the same site but were kept separate;
- social integration: the children mixed at social times, for example dinnertime; and
- academic integration: the children attended some of the classes with their peers.

There was a belief that there should be a continuum of provision to meet the needs of children with physical disabilities. Children with severe physical disabilities or complex needs were likely to attend special schools and even residential schools. Children with less severe difficulties could be at least partially integrated, often from a specially designated, resourced mainstream school. In addition, some children with mild physical disabilities were included in their local mainstream schools (*Within Reach* 1992). At the same time the categories of handicap were abolished and the concept of Special Educational Needs was introduced to describe the learning difficulties of a pupil. The focus in the 1980s was on recognising the differences between pupils – identifying their special educational needs. There are, however, no really accurate records on how children with physical disabilities were educated at this time. Neither LEAs nor central government have records on how many pupils with what kind of physical disability were educated in these different types of schools (*ibid.* 1992)

The development of inclusion

By the mid-1990s the term 'inclusion', as opposed to 'integration', was being used to describe the education of children with disabilities in mainstream schools. More recently, the term 'full' inclusion has been introduced (Giangreco 1997; Jarrett 1996). The full inclusion model has a number of features:

- all children attend the school to which they would go if they had no disabilities;
- a natural proportion of children with disabilities occurs at any school;
- no child should be excluded on the basis of a disability;
- school and general educational placements are age-appropriate, with no self-contained special educational classes operating on the school site;
- cooperative learning and peer teaching methods receive significant use in general teaching practice at the school; and
- special educational support teachers and TAs are provided within the context of the general educational class and other inclusive environments.

Full inclusion is not a reality in Britain. It is, however, an aspiration of some special educators and is used to promote changes. These changes in terminology, from handicapped to full inclusion, not only reflect special educators' concerns that children with special educational needs are not being appropriately educated, but they are also used to try and shift the public's perception of inclusion. In the last 50 years, teachers have been shown a variety of ways to most effectively educate children with physical disabilities. A fundamental principle of the government's present position set out in the Code of Practice is that: 'The special educational needs of children will normally be met in mainstream schools' (DfES 2001a: 7). However, it is clear that this is not intended to mean all children or full inclusion.

Throughout the book the term 'inclusion' will be used to describe the education of pupils with physical disabilities in mainstream schools. Inclusion will not mean 'full inclusion'; instead, it is recognised that inclusion can happen at a variety of levels in Britain today. Many schools feel constrained to offer full inclusion against the wishes of the parents and without appropriate support. Addressing these constraints in order to move to a position of full inclusion is the central concern of this book.

Answer the following questions using the scale: 4= strongly agree; 3= mildly agree; 2= mildly disagree; 1= strongly disagree.

Number	Item	Score
1	I feel that I have the knowledge to teach children with a physical disability.	
2	I support inclusion for children with physical disabilities.	
3	I feel that children with physical disabilities make better progress in mainstream than they would in special schools.	
4	I feel that children with physical disabilities are socially accepted by their peers.	
5	I feel that I am able to remediate the learning difficulties of children with a physical disability.	
6	I feel that children with physical disabilities benefit academically from inclusion in a mainstream classroom.	
7	I feel that other pupils benefit from the inclusion of children with physical disabilities into mainstream classrooms.	
8	I feel that I have adequate classroom support (TAs) for planning and working with these children.	
9	I believe that mainstream teachers should support inclusion as a positive education practice.	
10	I feel that adequate support services (such as speech and language therapists, physiotherapists, occupational therapists and educational psychologists) are readily available to me.	
11	I feel that children with physical disabilities get considerable support from their typical peers in the mainstream classroom.	
12	I am willing to attend additional INSET to broaden my knowledge about the education of children with physical disabilities.	
13	I feel that adequate equipment and teaching material is available to me for teaching children with physical disabilities.	
14	I feel that children with physical disabilities benefit socially from inclusion into a mainstream classroom.	
15	I believe that children with physical disabilities have a right to be in mainstream schools.	

Table 1.1   The teacher inclusion attitudes questionnaire (adapted from Sideridis and Chandler 1997)

Teachers' attitudes to inclusion

Teachers' attitudes to inclusion have a direct bearing on its success. The question-naire in Table 1.1 is designed to help teachers understand their own attitudes to inclusion. It can be completed by individual teachers or as part of a staff group.

Interpretation

The questionnaire can be broken down into five attitudes areas:

- **Rights** (questions 2, 9 and 15): teachers' beliefs about the right of children with physical disabilities to be included in mainstream schools;
- **Benefits** (questions 3, 6 and 14): teachers' beliefs about the academic and social benefits from inclusion for the pupil with a physical disability;
- **Skills** (questions 1, 5 and 12): teachers' beliefs about their skills and compe-tencies in effectively teaching and managing children with physical disabili-ties in mainstream schools;
- **Acceptance** (questions 4, 7 and 11): teachers' perceptions of the social accept-ance or rejection of pupils with a physical disability; and
- **Resources** (questions 8, 10 and 13): teachers' beliefs about the support given to the teacher in terms of resources, equipment and supportive personnel.

By adding the scores of the three questions in each area, a total score for each atti-tude is obtained (see Table 1.2).

The higher the score in each of these areas the more the teacher feels able and ready to include the child with a physical disability in her classroom. A score of 12 means that the teacher does not see any issues for inclusion in this area. However,

Attitude to inclusion	Total score
Rights	
Benefits	
Skills	
Acceptance	
Resources	

Table 1.2   Summary of attitude to inclusion

many teachers' will not give a score of 12 to each attitude area. Research has shown consistently that teachers have concerns in these five areas. However, before proceeding to look at these there are some further questions to think about:

- Which area am I most confident about (the one with the highest score)?
- Why do I feel confident in this area?
- Which areas do I feel least confident in? Why?
- Does everyone in the school feel the same way?
- Who sees it differently? Why?
- Have I always seen things this way? Why have things changed?
- What would need to happen for my beliefs to change in this area?

Thinking more about the five beliefs

There have been numerous studies looking at teachers' attitudes to inclusion. Most of these have taken place in the USA, Canada and Australia (Scruggs and Mastropieri 1996). However, some have taken place in Britain (Rose 2001). One of the most interesting things is that there is no relationship between the year in which the research was carried out and teachers' attitudes. In other words, teachers' attitudes have not changed significantly over the last 30 years despite all the historical changes in policy that have taken place. What, however, can be seen is that a positive attitude to inclusion is greater the further away the person is from the day-to-day responsibility for delivering it (Garvar-Pinhas and Schmelkin 1989). So, while policy-makers, administrators and university academics have increasingly argued the need for inclusion, teachers' views about inclusion have remained largely sceptical.

In the next section each of these beliefs is scrutinised in turn. They are scrutinised first in terms of what is known about the beliefs of mainstream teachers; then, for each belief, the background argument is set out to provide a framework in which to think about the particular belief.

1. Rights

Question: *Is it only just and right for children with physical disabilities to be included in mainstream schools?*
This belief is very much at the heart of inclusion. It is about whether teachers think inclusion is ethically right. Do children with physical disabilities have a right to be in a mainstream school? Generally speaking, the majority of teachers support the concept of inclusion (Scruggs and Mastropieri 1996). However, much depends on the severity of the physical disability; thus, in one study, 87 per cent of teachers

supported the inclusion of children with mild physical disabilities, for example a child who has some difficulties in moving around the school. However, only 32 per cent supported the inclusion of children with more severe physical disabilities, for example a child who is completely physically dependent (Berryman and Berryman 1981). So, though many teachers support the principle of inclusion, there is less support for the principle the greater the level of difficulty.

In practice, however, fewer mainstream teachers are actually willing to teach students with disabilities. The more additional responsibilities there are on the teachers the less willing they are to include the child (Scruggs and Mastropieri 1996). Most mainstream teachers believe they can teach children with mild physical difficulties, but under half are confident with children with moderate to severe physical disabilities (Phillips *et al.* 1990). Though most teachers believe inclusion is ethically right, a lower percentage are willing to teach children with special educational needs. This number goes down even further the more responsibilities are laid upon the teacher and the greater the severity of the disability.

The arguments for the right to inclusion
The rights, or social-justice, position underpins many of the arguments for inclusion (see Pearpoint *et al.* 1992). This politicises inclusion by contrasting it with segregation (Newell 1985). The issue of inclusion is linked to a broader perspective of discrimination; it is no longer simply about children with physical disabilities having their needs met; instead, inclusion is turned into a human rights issue. The focus becomes more than the interests of the individual child with a physical disability and more one in which the school, other children and society are on trial. The comparison is made between inclusion and institutional racism where individuals within an organisation, through their passive collusion, allow discrimination to take place.

This contrast with segregation changes the whole meaning of inclusion. It is no longer about how children with physical disabilities should have some time being educated with their peers. Inclusion means that children should be included in their local community schools all the time. Inclusion is seen as very different from integration (Thomas 1997). With integration, children had to prove their readiness to be integrated. With inclusion, the onus shifts to the schools and LEAs to prove their readiness to include. The tradition in Britain of providing a continuum of provision has come under criticism by groups such as the Alliance for Inclusive Education (Mason 1998).

Inclusion within this context is related to a definition of schools that includes all children within the community. The inclusion of children in mainstream school is now an international issue (Ainscow and Sebba 1996). The UNESCO World Conference on special educational needs, held in Salamanca in 1994, had a major influence on the perception of inclusion as a human rights issue. The conference's

Statement and Framework for Action included the right of children with special educational needs to have access to regular schools.

At present, the argument centres on the appropriateness of the full inclusion model built around a continuum of services within the mainstream classroom, or the appropriateness of a continuum of provision, ranging from full inclusion to a residential special school.

The main moral argument for the continuum of provision is a denial of the uniqueness of each child and families' needs (Skinner 1996). The argument is that there is never one 'right' solution to all difficulties – that there is no magic solution. Therefore, to restrict the options of education to mainstream schooling is a denial of the individual rights of the child. The second argument is that to equate discrimination in terms of race to that of disability is to trivialise the needs of students with disabilities to have specialised accommodation and facilities (Fuchs and Fuchs 1995).

The third argument against inclusion is that some parents of children with physical disabilities do not want it. This is recognised by the British government in the DfEE's 1997 Green Paper. Though the principle of inclusion is endorsed, there is a clear recognition that some pupils will not be included into mainstream schools. The concerns of parents are highlighted:

> We recognise the concerns of some parents about whether and how the needs of their child will be met in mainstream school . . . Parents will continue to have the right to express a preference for a special school where they consider this appropriate to their child's needs. (p. 45)

Following the consultation process, *Meeting Special Educational Needs: A Programme for Action* (DfEE 1998) confirmed the government's position: 'Promoting inclusion within mainstream schools, where parents want it and appropriate support can be provided, will remain the cornerstone of our strategy' (p. 13). This statement highlights the government's view that, though inclusion is desirable, full inclusion is not the way forward until all parents are happy with mainstream schools.

Chapter 3 highlights the differences between parents and teachers on the most basic issues of inclusive education. These issues include the appropriateness of mainstream placement, the content of the curriculum and the criteria for deciding levels of provision. Parents and educators do not have a shared framework on which to base decisions or actions (Giangreco 1997).

The main effect of the right to full inclusion position is to act as a catalyst for change: placing inclusion in the context of human rights has forced teachers to ask not if inclusion is a good thing, but how can it actually work so that it benefits all the pupils?

Summary
It is only just and right for children with physical disabilities to be included when:

- teachers support such inclusion;
- parents support such inclusion; and
- appropriate support can be provided.

2. Benefits

Question: *Do children with physical disabilities benefit academically and socially from inclusion?*
One of the main reasons that teachers and parents may not support inclusion is that they believe it is not academically or socially beneficial to the child. Most teachers think inclusion is of some benefit; however, most do not believe that it is necessarily the most beneficial placement for the child with special education needs. Only a minority of mainstream class teachers think that full-time inclusion will produce the most academic and social benefits relative to a special class placement (Scruggs and Mastropieri 1996). The importance of this is that expectations actually influence educational practice and outcomes (Stolber *et al.* 1998). In other words, the teacher's *beliefs* about whether there are benefits for the child actually *affects* whether there are benefits. What then is the evidence for the benefits of including children with a physical disability?

The argument for the benefits of inclusion
The research on the benefits of inclusion is divided into two parts: the first part is concerned with what evidence there is to show that all children with SEN who are included do better, academically and socially, than they would in a special school; the second part looks at what evidence there is that children with physical disabilities do better in mainstream.

Benefits of inclusion for children with SEN
There are significant methodological difficulties in evaluating the benefits of inclusion (Farrell 1997). In particular, there are difficulties of generalisation from children often with very specific individual needs. Also there are differences in provision which makes comparisons difficult. Finally, there are the vested interests of the researchers. One way of making some general conclusions about the benefits of inclusion is by carrying out a meta-analysis of the research. A meta-analysis combines information from a number of studies to see if individual studies support each other. This reduces the dangers inherent in just looking at small studies which may be biased due to the particular provision or the type of children being looked at.

Three meta-analyses summarise the research on inclusion. These studies produced a common measure known as the effect size. This is the effect that inclusion has over special education. The results are summarised in Table 1.3.

These meta-analytic reviews of the research show 'a small-to-moderate beneficial effect of inclusive education on the academic and social outcomes of special-needs children' (Baker *et al.* 1995). All of the effect sizes were positive, showing that children educated in mainstream classes do better academically and socially than comparable children in special classes and schools. The authors conclude that the effects of inclusion are positive and worthwhile but that they are not huge. These large meta-analyses do, therefore, provide some general support for the idea that inclusion is beneficial both academically and socially for children with special educational needs.

Benefits of inclusion for children with a physical disability

There have been very few studies specifically on evaluating the effectiveness of the inclusion of children with physical disabilities into mainstream school. One of the first studies showed that inclusion could be successful, academically, given appropriate intellectual ability and articulation skills (Bowley 1969). Another early study showed that children with a mild physical disability and average intellectual ability had a range of problems, including being teased about their physical disabilities (Marlow *et al.* 1968).

Anderson's (1973, 1975) research was the first detailed analysis of the inclusion of primary-age children with physical disabilities in Britain. She found that the great majority of children with a physical disability were happy at mainstream school. However, they had fewer friends. Her research demonstrated that children with physical disabilities could be effectively included in mainstream schools.

Author(s)	Carlberg and Kavale	Wang and Baker	Baker
Year published	1980	1985–6	1994
Time period	pre-1980	1975–84	1983–92
Number of studies	50	11	13
Academic effect size	0.15	0.44	0.08
Social effect size	0.11	0.11	0.28

Table 1.3   The effects of inclusive placement

However, she recommended a cautious approach to inclusion with a careful consideration of the type of physical disability the child had.

By the early 1980s educators were urging caution in the inclusion of pupils with physical disabilities into mainstream school. Center and Ward (1984) argued that, despite the 'rights' argument, there was little research to show which children actually benefited from inclusion in academic or social terms. Nor had the prerequisites in terms of teacher skills and attitudes been identified. Their research, in Australia, investigated the effective inclusion of children with mild cerebral palsy (CP). They found, on average, that the children had lower scores, on various tests of reading and maths achievement and social acceptability, than the rest of the mainstream children. However, the children with CP were not a homogeneous group. There were a significant number of these children who were doing very well both academically and socially. In addition, there was no comparison with how similar children would have achieved if they were placed in a special school. They concluded that children with physical disabilities could not be guaranteed success in a mainstream school until various support systems were in place. In particular, they recommended:

- provision of early educational intervention;
- liaison between preschool facilities and mainstream schools;
- teacher preparation;
- resources; and
- community participation.

Center *et al.* (1991) developed this research with an important and detailed two-staged study of the characteristics of children, classrooms and schools which promote effective inclusion. Their research showed that children with physical disabilities were almost all well integrated unless they had multiple difficulties. Children with multiple difficulties were largely unsuccessful at being integrated. However, the authors suggested that it was unwise to assume that it was simply the severity of the physical disability that accounted for successful or unsuccessful inclusion. There were wide differences in the severity of disability that the children had that were successfully included.

Most importantly, the research showed that successful inclusion depended on structured teaching and the appropriateness of support. If teachers used a structured teaching style, and if appropriate support was provided, then primary children could be successfully included irrespective of the type or severity of their physical disability. Vice versa, without these two factors, pupils were unable to be integrated successfully. The only exception to this was if the school showed a very positive school ethos in terms of their commitment to inclusion. If this was demonstrated they might be able to, at least partially, overcome the lack of structured teaching or provision.

The significance of the research is that it stresses that successful inclusion is not about within-pupil factors, but is about the effectiveness of the teaching and the school organisation and ethos.

Summary
Children with physical disabilities benefit academically and socially from attending mainstream schools when:

- there is a positive school ethos;
- the teacher uses a structured style of teaching; and
- the teacher has appropriate support.

3. Skills

Question: *Do teachers have the necessary skills and knowledge for successful inclusion?*
The third area is about how teachers perceive their competence in effectively teaching and managing children with physical disabilities in mainstream schools.

The majority of teachers believe that significant changes in terms of classroom procedures, teaching and curriculum are necessary to accommodate children with special educational needs (Scruggs and Mastropieri 1996). Most mainstream teachers do not believe that they have sufficient expertise to promote inclusion; nor do they believe that they are sufficiently trained or prepared (Rose 2001). However, teachers do not believe simply with training that they would have the necessary skills and knowledge to include children with physical disabilities.

The argument for the skills of the teacher
There is considerable debate around whether teachers need specialist skills for teaching children with physical disabilities. On one side of the argument are teachers who believe that they do not have the appropriate skills. On the other are educators who make the argument that effective teachers do not require specialist or different skills to teach children with special needs. The research outlined in the previous section is a helpful starting point. Center *et al.* (1991) showed that a central factor for successful inclusion is a structured teaching style. (The other factor, the appropriateness of support, will be dealt with in the section on resources.) A structured teaching style is defined by having the following components:

- clear presentation of lessons;
- provision of a lesson outline;
- presentation of step-by-step, sequenced lesson directions;

- direct teaching in basic skill areas;
- regular monitoring of the child's basic skills;
- the provision of continuous feedback to children about oral or written work; and
- the teacher's active involvement with children during seatwork.

This structured teaching style has also been identified as that of effective mainstream teachers (Wittrock 1985). Previous research had elaborated on some of these areas (Larrivee 1985). For example, the type of feedback that the children require has been shown to be:

- positive feedback for correct response;
- prompting to encourage response;
- rephrasing or providing cues for incorrect response;
- infrequent criticism.

Lessons need to be structured so that:

- there is little time wasted in transition between activities;
- there is high time on the activity; and
- activities are provided at the appropriate level.

Once again, these are all factors that apply to effective teaching in the mainstream classroom. The research clearly shows that the skills required for teaching children with SEN effectively are exactly those required to teach all children. However, many teachers do not feel that they have sufficient skills. There are a number of reasons for this:

Cultural: for a long time teachers were told that children with physical disabilities needed to be taught in schools that were special.

Multiprofessional: teachers recognise that these children have other developmental needs – for example physical or communication – that require input from other professionals.

Communication: children with physical disabilities can have difficulties communicating. Even if these needs are primarily addressed by a multiprofessional team (for example with input from speech and language therapists), teachers are often concerned about how they may need to adapt their communication.

Ability: because of their physical and communication disability teachers may believe that the child has learning difficulties that they cannot meet in the classroom.

Unfamiliarity: there are aspects of working with children with physical disabilities which are unfamiliar to the teacher. These may include terminology (e.g. scoliosis), equipment (e.g. communication boards) and classroom adaptations (e.g. adjustable desk). This unfamiliarity leads teachers to think that different teaching skills are also required to teach these children.

Some of these issues can be addressed through training. However, training is most effective if focused on a particular child rather than being done theoretically (Lipsky and Gartner 1996). There is also an argument that experience may be more important than training (Ainscow 1999). This is supported by Larrivee (1985), who showed that the greater the teacher's length of experience with children with SEN, the more they had the characteristics of the effective structured teaching. Most effective for teachers is a mentoring or coaching system. This allows an experienced teacher (of children with physical disabilities) to provide support and advice to their less experienced colleagues.

Summary
Teachers have the skills and knowledge for effective inclusion when they:

- structure their teaching;
- provide effective feedback;
- present activities at the appropriate level and maintain motivation;
- have effective multidisciplinary support in non-education development areas; and
- reflect on their own experience of teaching children with physical disabilities with the help of a mentor.

4. Acceptance

Question: *Will the inclusion of a child with physical disabilities have a negative effect on the rest of the class?*
Many teachers are concerned that the child with a physical disability will not be accepted by his peers. They worry that the child may be isolated and have few friends. They are also concerned that the child may take attention away from other pupils thus causing them to be resentful. This might also be a cause of resentment by parents who may believe their children's progress may suffer as the result of the inclusion of a child with physical disabilities (Rose 2001).

The arguments for social acceptance
There have been a number of studies comparing the progress of all the children in an inclusive class with that of matched children in a class which does not include

any disabled children. These studies consistently show that the non-disabled children's progress is not affected by having a child with physical disabilities in the class as long as the class is appropriately resourced (Staub and Peck 1995).

There are, however, also potential benefits for inclusion in terms of social acceptance. In primary classes containing children with disabilities there is a reduced fear of children who look and act differently. Both primary school children and their parents become less fearful (York and Tundidor 1995). There also appears to be an increase in self-esteem and a reduction in prejudice for many able-bodied children as a result of their relationships with disabled children (Peck *et al.* 1992). These early relationships can grow into warm and caring long-term friendships (Staub and Peck 1995).

This is not to minimise the difficulties that children with physical disabilities can have in being socially accepted. Parents' major concern when their child with a physical disability starts school is whether their child will make friends (Fox 1999). Prejudice against anyone who is different is a common phenomenon and the influence of the teacher is crucial in overcoming prejudice (Parish *et al.* 1980). Children with physical disabilities may have difficulties making friends and this needs to be facilitated by the teacher (Strully and Strully 1989).

Booth *et al.* (1997) have highlighted the present dilemma for schools. The government's insistence on raising expectations and standards does not at first sight square easily with inclusion. The school has to convince parents that including children with physical disabilities will not disadvantage their child's education. The above research goes further than this, suggesting that this diversity, far from being damaging, can actually be beneficial to all pupils.

Summary
The inclusion of a child with physical disabilities will have a positive effect on the rest of the class by:

- reinforcing a structured teaching approach;
- promoting the acceptance of difference;
- reducing fear and prejudice; and
- increasing the self-esteem of all the children.

5. Resources

Question: *Are additional resources or support required for the successful inclusion of children with physical disabilities?*
Resources can be divided into material resources, such as appropriate equipment or teaching material, and personnel resources, such as TAs and other professionals (e.g. physiotherapists). Teachers believe that inclusion creates work that requires

additional time (Barton 1992). This time can be given by TAs. However, most teachers do not believe that they have a satisfactory amount of TA time (Rose 2001). Teachers believe that they have better support with equipment and material than with personnel support (Scruggs and Mastropieri 1996).

The arguments for resources

Underpinning the resource issue is one of time (Stolber *et al.* 1998). There are a range of reasons why teachers need time to include pupils with a physical disability. Time is needed to:

- provide individual teaching, for example with a language or physical management programme;
- support the child accessing the teaching activity;
- support the transition between learning activities; and
- facilitate independence skills.

(adapted from Rose 2001)

In order to do the above, additional time is required to:

- plan a well-defined curriculum;
- plan and work with the TA;
- plan and work with other professionals, for example physiotherapists; and
- plan and attend meetings with parents.

(Logan and Malone 1998; Thomas *et al.* 1998; Bennett *et al.* 1997)

Classroom support from a TA is the key strategy by which this time can be created. Though there is some regional and local variation (in terms of delegation of budgets to schools) the resources for children with physical disabilities remains closely tied to the child's statements issued by the LEA. However, there has been increasing pressure on LEAs' resources in the last decade. First of all, there has been a consistent increase in the number of children with statements of special educational needs. In addition, the percentage of children with new statements placed in mainstream schools has risen each year. In 1995, 66.4 per cent of all new statements were placed in mainstream school, and by 2000 this figure had risen to 75.6 per cent (DfES 2001c).

There are, therefore, an increasing proportion of pupils in mainstream schools who are statemented and using LEA resources. Budgeting within LEAs means that these resources need to be spread more thinly to meet these children's needs.

The efficient management of resources is a central issue which underpins inclusion (Society of Education Officers 1996). The last report by the DES (1989), specifically on educating pupils with physical difficulties, highlighted the diverse range of educational placements that LEAs were using. These ranged from special schools to inclusion into mainstream schools. The report highlighted that many

LEAs were at that time reviewing their provision and the efficient use of resources was a significant feature of these reviews. At this time the inclusion of individual children in mainstream schools was queried as an efficient use of resources.

Two other factors compound the issues of resources. The first is that of the accessibility of the school. Despite SENDA (DfES 2001b), many schools are not fully accessible for someone in a wheelchair. If a school has not been made accessible, resources will be required to undertake the necessary adaptations. Without significant capital investment in buildings many pupils with physical disabilities will not have access to inclusion (see Chapter 8 for further implications on schools' Accessibility Plans).

The second factor that compounds the issue of resources is that other agencies are involved in the provision of resources for children with physical disabilities. In particular, the NHS, through the local trusts, provides professionals essential for inclusion – physiotherapists, occupational therapists and speech and language therapists. They are also responsible for some of the equipment, for example communication aids. The involvement of these other agencies means that resourcing decisions can be particularly problematic.

The above highlights the difficulties that teachers may have accessing appropriate support for the inclusion of the child with a physical disability. Teachers recognise these resource pressures on LEAs and schools. However, they also believe that effective inclusion for children with physical disabilities depends on additional resources. The President of the American Federation of Teachers (USA) suggested that teachers should have a duty to report failures to provide services and should be offered protection from reprisal for this type of whistle-blowing. The ability of teachers to protect the interests of children with statements, where stated provision is not provided, is presently very unclear.

Summary
Additional resources, as supported by SENDA, are required for the successful inclusion of children with physical disabilities in order to:

- adapt the school building;
- provide NHS support for specific needs – particularly the physical management programme;
- provide specialist equipment;
- provide teaching assistants; and
- allow the teacher to plan successfully.

The role of the teacher

This chapter has examined the attitude of teachers to the inclusion of children with physical disabilities. It starts from the premise that it is the teacher's beliefs that underpin successful inclusion.

Inclusion can only work with the initial support of the head teacher. The head teacher effectively serves as the gatekeeper to the school. If he or she does not support inclusion it will not happen. It is the head teacher who provides the enthusiasm and moral support for inclusion both as a concept and as a reality.

If it is the head teacher who effectively decides if inclusion is going to happen, it is the class teacher who decides if it is a success or a failure (Erwin and Soodak 1995). It is the class teacher's attitudes which actually make inclusion a success. The central belief is that most primary teachers support the inclusion of children with physical disabilities in principle. The difficulties lie in a number of key areas. Knowing the research in these areas provides a basis for reflecting on present beliefs.

Adults can take up a variety of roles about inclusion depending on their beliefs and the situation in which they find themselves. Four modes have been identified:

- resignation mode
- championing mode
- mentoring mode
- normalisation mode

Resignation mode

Some teachers are fatalistic, believing nothing can change to help the inclusion of a child with physical disabilities in their class. They find that teaching takes all their energies. They may be unsupported in their school, be new to teaching or have seen it all before. In addition, they may have a range of other children with special education needs in their class.

Championing mode

Some teachers act as champions for inclusion. They believe that children with physical disabilities have a right to be included. In order for this to happen they believe there is the necessity for change. This may involve change for the individual child; for example a change in their physical management programme. It may also involve change at the school level; for example attitudes to disability; or at the LEA level, in how resources are allocated. Such teachers get involved in challenging the status quo on behalf of the child and their family and the school. The goal of this championing is inclusion.

Mentoring mode

Some teachers have considerable experience of the inclusion of children with physical disabilities. They use this experience to support colleagues new to such challenges. This support can be in terms of specific advice on equipment or teaching strategies or it can take more the form of emotional support for teachers in the resignation mode. Such active involvement by these teachers, long after their own direct involvement, with a child with a physical disability is vital. They will often be seen to have an unofficial leadership role in terms of inclusion. They make a choice to remain involved.

Normalisation mode

Some teachers take a normalisation mode. In fact, all teachers take a normalising role for most children – they believe they should be included as a normal part of the school. For some teachers this normalisation process would include children who were left-handed (once seen as an educational problem), slightly clumsy or had difficulties of movement down one side of their body. Other teachers take this normalisation process to include all children who use wheelchairs. The point is that different teachers have different expectations about what is normal. These expectations may change during the course of the school year. So a child who at the beginning of the year is seen as disabled may by the end of the year be seen as just one of the class.

These four roles are a helpful way of conceptualising how teachers take up very different positions as regards inclusion. They are not personality types but rather roles that a teacher can take on. The same teacher may take on different roles depending on the school in which they are. All the roles have a functional purpose and can be a completely valid response to a particular situation. The resignation role has the function of identifying teachers who feel under considerable stress and need support and empowerment. It is hoped that this book can help teachers shift roles and move from resignation to championing to mentoring and normalisation.

Summary

Teachers' expectations are the basis for the successful inclusion of the child with a physical disability. Five basic assertions can be made:

- **Rights:** It is only right and proper for children with physical disabilities to be included in mainstream schools.
- **Benefits:** Children with physical disabilities benefit academically and socially from attending mainstream schools.

- **Skills:** Teachers do have the knowledge and skills for successful inclusion.
- **Acceptance:** The inclusion of a child with a physical disability will have a positive effect on their peers.
- **Resources:** Additional resources or support are required for the successful inclusion of children with physical disabilities.

This chapter has shown that all the above statements are true under certain conditions. The rest of the book examines how these conditions can be met in mainstream schools.

CHAPTER 2

What Are Physical Disabilities?

Difficulties or disability?

What is meant by the term 'physical disability'? Chapter 1 outlines how the words used to describe children with a disability have changed over the years – from 'handicapped' to 'having special educational needs'. There continues to be considerable debate about which words are most appropriate to use. Language reflects and shapes the way people think about physical disability, and this can be illustrated in a small but important way: some people talk about the child with a disability, which implies that the child has the disability. Other people prefer to use the term 'the disabled child'; this implies that the child is disabled by the situation around him – for example people's attitudes and lack of resources rather than by any physical difficulties he may have. This chapter focuses on the child's physical difficulties. Whether they are physically disabled will depend on how schools and other services manage these difficulties.

There are a number of other common words and phrases that can handicap

Try to avoid	Use instead
Handicapped child	Disabled child
Suffers from, a victim of	Has the condition, has the impairment
Confined to a wheelchair Wheelchair bound	Wheelchair-user
Mentally handicapped Learning disabled	Learning difficulty
Crippled	Disabled child
Spastic	Has cerebral palsy

Table 2.1   Handicapping words

physically disabled children. The words on the left are seen to portray the child with a physical disability as a passive victim who needs help. Scope (1998) has produced a useful guide to what is appropriate to use at the present time (see Table 2.1). However, remember that the use of these words will also change and will need to be modified in the future.

Physical difficulties – a continuum

The term 'physical disabilities' is a label – one that covers a vast range of difficulties to do with physical functioning. But how broad a continuum is this? There is little doubt that compared with an Olympic athlete most people would be considered to have physical difficulties. At one end of the continuum there are children with minor motor problems; at the other are children who have little control over their physical functioning. However, in between there are a whole range of difficulties. Does a pupil who is poorly coordinated or who is clumsy have physical difficulties? What about a pupil who is in a wheelchair but has perfect coordination? What about the same pupil who is recovering from a road traffic accident and will be walking again within six months? All these pupils have difficulties with their physical functioning. These difficulties may be about the range of physical movements a child can do; for example, they cannot walk. Or it can be about the ease with which they can do it, e.g. they can walk but it takes much longer than it does for most children.

The child's physical difficulties turn into a disability if it prevents him – disables him – from participating in society in general and school in particular. The child who is poorly coordinated may be physically disabled because he is unable to complete the coursework required for an examination course. However, the same child, provided with a word processor and appropriate software, may no longer be physically disabled even if he has the same physical difficulties.

This book is largely focused on those pupils whose physical difficulties make them feel disabled at present in mainstream schools. What is presently considered a physical disability may not be ten years from now. For example, children with what are now considered minor difficulties, for example a hip problem, could in the past have been considered disabled and been sent to a special school. At present, a child having any of the following difficulties may mean that he is considered as being physical disabled:

- moving around the school;
- moving within the classroom;
- positioning within a lesson;
- accessing the curriculum in terms of hand skills;

Physical Skills: checklist for teachers

Please complete each section

Areas of physical difficulties

Mobility	Tick one
Walks fluently	
Can walk but not fluent	
Difficulties with walking with reduced mobility	
No independent walking	
Uses wheelchair to help with mobility?	

Head control	Tick one
Normal head control	
Difficulties – but can hold head up for extended periods of time	
Difficulties – can hold head up for very short periods of time	
No obvious head control	
Uses adapted seating to help with head control?	

Sitting	Tick one
No apparent problem when sitting on normal chair	
Can sit unsupported but not secure or stable	
Can not be left sitting unless supported	
Difficult to place or maintain in a sitting position even with support	
Uses adapted seating to help with positioning?	

Using hands	Tick one
No apparent problems with using both hands together	
Some difficulties with using both hands together but can dress self (age-appropriate)	
Can pick up and hold pencil	
Unable to reach and grasp	
Uses switch system to access curriculum?	

Table 2.2 Physical skills: checklist for teachers (adapted from Evans *et al.* 1989)

Speech	Tick one
No problem with articulation of speech	
Some difficulties with understanding speech	
Unable to understand speech	
Uses adapted or augmentative equipment to aid communication?	

In addition, it is helpful to have the following information:

Observed unwanted movements	At rest	With excitement or goal-directed activity
None		
Short and jerky		
Slow and writhing		
Tremor		
Muscle spasms		

Distribution of physical difficulties	Yes	No	Uncertain
Are there obvious differences between the two sides of the body?			
If yes, which side is better?			
Are the arms more affected than the legs?			
Are the legs more affected than the arms?			

Summary: the child has physical difficulties in the following areas:

Sub-area	Yes	No	Don't know	Equipment used/ required	Comments
Mobility					
Head control					
Sitting					
Using hands					
Speech					

Table 2.2   *Continued*

- accessing the curriculum because of speech difficulties due to physical difficulties.

A teacher should always know a child's functional physical skills as a basis for understanding the child physical needs in the classroom. Completing the 'Physical skills: checklist for teachers' (Table 2.2) is a useful basis for this understanding.

Different types of physical difficulties

Children's physical difficulties stem from different conditions, or what are known as medical syndromes. These syndromes are often, though not always, diagnosed before the child starts school. The issue about the diagnosis of a syndrome is that it is a simplification. This simplification can be a convenient shorthand for describing a child. So instead of just using the term 'the child with physical difficulties', it is helpful to know the medical diagnosis of the child. There are significant differences between the education of a child with cerebral palsy and one with muscular dystrophy. However, every child with the same medical diagnosis does not have the same educational needs. Teachers need to understand the implications of the medical diagnosis and then see behind the diagnosis for the implications for this particular child.

Understanding the diagnosis is helpful in a number of ways. It helps the teacher:

- liaise with other professionals who will use this label;
- discuss issues with the parents in a knowledgeable way;
- be more aware of why certain activities are beneficial and why others are not;
- be sensitive to secondary problems, for example tiredness.

Given that there is no clear definition of what physical difficulties are there can be no precise figure about the number of children with physical difficulties in the school population. However, it is possible to give some indication of the types. There are three main conditions that children with physical difficulties may have:

- cerebral palsy – 1 in every 400 children
- spina bifida – 1 in every 300/1,000 (N.B. regional variations)
- muscular dystrophy – 1 in every 3,000 children (virtually always boys)

In addition, there are a whole range of uncommon genetic conditions which can also affect the child's physical skills, e.g. brittle bone disease (1 in every 20,000 births).

Physical difficulties are all difficulties with movements. However, these difficulties can stem from different areas. In particular:

- the centres in the brain for controlling motor movements (e.g. cerebral palsy);

- the neural tube, which sends the information from the brain to the muscles (e.g. spina bifida);
- the muscles themselves (e.g. muscular dystrophy).

Keeping these differences in mind helps the understanding of the different strengths and difficulties the pupil may have.

Cerebral palsy

Cerebral palsy (CP) is an umbrella term that covers a group of conditions. What these conditions have in common is that they are present from birth and arise from difficulties the child's brain has in controlling bodily movements: 'Cerebral palsy is the name given to a group of conditions in which there is a disturbance in the way the brain controls the muscles of the body' (Queensland Spastic Welfare League 1993). This definition highlights that the difficulties are due to a 'disturbance' in the brain. This word is much more helpful than older definitions that referred to the child being brain-damaged. It is important to acknowledge that the child's difficulties with movement stem from a disturbance in the brain and that this has educational implications. A helpful analogy is between the brain and a filing cabinet. Sometimes there is difficulty in retrieving information from a filing cabinet. This may be because the filing cabinet has been damaged, but it is more likely to be that the indexing system is not working properly. In a similar way the child with cerebral palsy can be seen to have difficulties retrieving information and sending it to the right muscles in the body rather than the brain being damaged.

Causes of cerebral palsy

One of the reasons for stressing the above is that there was a widely held view that cerebral palsy is caused by 'brain damage' due to asphyxia at birth. It is now believed that asphyxia at birth is the cause of about 10 per cent of cerebral palsy. Much more likely to have CP are preterm babies who are very vulnerable because of their size. Over a third of babies with CP are preterm. With the advances in medical technology it is likely that this number may rise.

Parts of the body affected

Cerebral palsy can affect different parts of the body:

- quadriplegia means all four limbs are affected – and usually the trunk too;
- diplegia means that only two limbs are affected – usually the legs. This is also known as paraplegia;
- hemiplegia means only one side of the body is affected.

These words are often used as part of the general description of the child's physical difficulties. There are, however, usually differences in how much individual limbs are affected. For example, a child may be quadriplegic (i.e. all four limbs affected) but may find it much easier to use his right rather than his left hand. Knowing which hand, or leg, the child has greater control over may be a key to the successful use of switches.

What type of cerebral palsy?
Three types of CP have been identified: spastic, athetosis and ataxia. Each of these has different physical characteristics (Levitt 1982).

Spastic
This is the most common form of cerebral palsy. The physical characteristics are:

- tightness: muscle tension (hypertonus) leads to clasp-knife-type reactions as muscles contract.
- abnormal postures: tight muscle groups often hold the body in an abnormal position. This can lead to fixed deformities or contractures, for example of the spine (scoliosis). The child needs to be correctly positioned and repositioned.
- changes in muscles tension: muscle tension (hypertonus) may be affected by changes in position, especially of the head and neck. It will also be increased by sudden movements and changes in the child's emotional state (excitement or fear).
- voluntary movement: the child's limbs are not paralysed but they may be very difficult to move and not have the full range of movements. He may take a particularly long time to start movements.

Athetosis
The physical characteristics are:

- involuntary movements: children with athetosis have purposeless movements. These may be of a variety of forms but are often writhing. They have a great deal of difficulty controlling their movements.
- conscious control: paradoxically, these movements are increased by trying to control them. Heightened emotion (excitement or fear) will also increase the athetosis. When the child is relaxed through focusing on something else there is a decrease in the involuntary movements.
- changes with time: the involuntary movements may only appear at 2 or 3 years of age.

Ataxia
The physical characteristics are:

- difficulties with balance: children with ataxia often can walk, but their

movements are unsteady and they have poor balance. They have particular difficulties when moving around the school or at break times.
- voluntary movements: the child may move when they want to but there are coordination problems. The child often appears clumsy with poor fine motor control and an intentional tremor.

The above descriptions are a useful starting point for understanding some of the issues for children with cerebral palsy. However, it is important to recognise that for each individual child there may be a combination of physical characteristics, with each limb affected to a greater or lesser extent.

Specific implications for teachers
- Cerebral palsy is a static condition. Children should not lose any practical skills during their school career. They will however require a physical management programme to maintain and develop physical skills.
- They are most likely to gain physical skills up until age 7 approximately.
- Cerebral palsy is based on difficulties the brain has in controlling movement. These difficulties may affect other aspects of education. In particular, they may affect visual-perceptual skills.
- Children with cerebral palsy may also have difficulties controlling the muscles in their mouth. This means they may have difficulties with their speech.

Spina bifida

The second most common physical condition is spina bifida. Spina bifida means 'split spine', and is due to the neural tube failing to develop completely and close. This means that surgery is required soon after birth to close the spinal lesion. There are a number of different types of spina bifida. Some types, once operated on, have little or no long-term effects while others lead to considerable physical difficulties.

The location of the spinal lesion is the key to understanding the extent of the difficulties. If the lesion is at the bottom of the back, it is likely that the child can walk, though he may have bladder and bowel difficulties. If the lesion is below the ribs, the child may need braces and crutches to walk. However, if the lesion is higher, then the child may be paraplegic and may not be able to walk (Rekate 1990).

Frequently, the child with spina bifida may also have difficulties with the circulation of fluid between the spinal column and the brain. This can result in enlargement of the brain, which is called hydrocephalus. This is commonly known as 'water on the brain' and occurs in approximately 80 per cent of children with spina bifida cystica. To clear this, an operation is often undertaken to insert a 'shunt' into the brain cavity. This is a small plastic catheter which allows the fluid to drain off. It is a simple operation but there are often ongoing problems with shunts, including infections and malfunctioning.

Specific implications for teachers
- Spina bifida is a static condition and the child should not lose any functional skills while at school. If the child appears to deteriorate, it is important to alert parents and the medical authorities, as there may be difficulties with the shunt.
- Children with spina bifida will require a programme of physical management. Young children will be encouraged to walk. However, by the age of 6, if the child cannot stand unaided, it is unlikely he will be able to learn to walk without help. A decision is often taken at that stage to focus on the mobility using a wheelchair (Hall and Hill 1996).
- Pressure sores are a real problem and the child needs to be regularly repositioned in class. In addition, the child must learn to position and reposition himself to prevent these sores.
- Many children with spina bifida have difficulties with toileting. There needs to be a regular toileting programme in school with a consistent time to establish regular bowel movements. Urinary infection is a serious problem for children with spina bifida and, therefore, a hygiene programme also needs to be incorporated into the day.

Muscular dystrophy

Muscular dystrophy is an inherited disease of the muscles and is fatal. The most common form is Duchenne, which is only very rarely seen in girls. The incidence in boys is about one in 3,000 births. There is a progressive breakdown of muscle fibres with a consequent increasing weakness and loss of muscle bulk. It is often not noted until the child is between 2 and 4 years of age and it may not be formally diagnosed for another few years. Initially, the child may have difficulty running or climbing steps, but soon he develops difficulties walking, and by age 12 he is likely to have to use a wheelchair. There are differences in how fast muscular dystrophy progresses, but most children do not survive into adulthood.

Specific implications for teachers
- The child will become increasingly aware of his condition during these early years. It is important that he receives good emotional support.
- Teachers may also find this very challenging. They also need to receive emotional support and counselling when they feel they need it.
- Attention needs to be given to planning. Part of this will be concerned with mobility and transferring from walking to being in a wheelchair. A clear programme of physical management needs to be in place.
- Once the child stops walking there is a high risk of contractures and deformities. The child needs to be involved in planning a programme for physical management which recognises their ambitions and motivation.

Genetic conditions

There are a large number of children with physical disabilities who do not have any of the above diagnoses. They are likely to have a rare, but diagnosed, condition or an unknown condition. There are literally hundreds of different physical conditions; some of these are very rare with maybe only a few hundred children in the whole of Britain who have the condition. For others there is, as yet, no known diagnosis. This is changing rapidly, with advances in DNA testing making it easier to specify the basis for the physical difficulty. These medical changes mean that some children who were diagnosed with more common conditions, such as cerebral palsy, are now being rediagnosed.

Implications for teachers
- If you have not heard of the condition, ask the SENCO or the school nurse about it.
- Use the internet as a source to gather information on these rare conditions.
- Share your observations and experiences (while ensuring anonymity for the child). Gradually, a better picture will build up among professionals about some of the educational aspects of these rare conditions.

Secondary difficulties

A number of these conditions are directly related to the developing brain, in particular cerebral palsy. This means that there are a variety of other neurological difficulties associated with physical disabilities. Three of these difficulties are particularly important: vision, hearing and epilepsy. A child with physical difficulties may have all or none of these secondary difficulties. What is important is that teachers check whether the child is affected by any of these difficulties.

Vision

Children with physical difficulties are also more likely to have visual difficulties than are their peers. A distinction is made between impairments of vision due to disorders of visual input and problems which arise with processing visual information (Dutton *et al.* 1999). The visual difficulties the child has may be compounded by his physical difficulties. So a child's limited independent movement will also limit his opportunities for visual stimulation.

Visual input
Visual difficulties are normally assessed along two dimensions (Lodge 1999):

- visual acuity (clarity of vision); and
- visual field (peripheral vision).

Visual acuity describes how clearly an object is seen. Normal visual acuity is between 20/20 and 20/40. A child with 20/20 vision can see perfectly at a distance of 20 feet. A child with 20/40 vision can see at 20 feet what most children can see at 40 feet. A normal field of vision is defined as between 160 and 180 degrees on the horizontal plane, and 120 degrees on the vertical plane. A child who has this visual field restricted is said to have 'tunnel' vision, as it is like looking down a tunnel.

Children are considered visually impaired if their visually acuity or visual field is less than these standards. A child is considered blind if his visual acuity is 20/200 (i.e. he cannot see at 20 feet what most children can see at 200 feet) in his worst eye, with glasses, and/or if his horizontal visual field is 20 degrees or less.

If the child has a problem with visual acuity he is likely to have a difficulty with educational activities. For example, he will not be able to see printed words clearly. If the child has a visual field difficulty, he is likely to have difficulties with mobility and movement around the classroom or school.

Children with physical difficulties are also particularly prone to problems controlling and coordinating the movement of the eyeballs. This can lead to: **nystagmus**, where there is involuntary, rapid, side-to-side or up and down movement of the eyes; **strabismus**, where the two eyes are not aligned with each other; this results in cross-eyes where the two eyes cannot look at the same time at one object; and **amblyopia** (lazy eye), where the child suppresses the use of one of his eyes. These conditions can cause eye fatigue and headaches if the child overextends himself, for example through reading (Lodge 1999).

There are a very small number of children with severe visual and physical difficulties. With such children the class teacher will require considerable extra resources and specialist support from the visually impaired specialists within the area. Completing the 'Visual input: checklist for teachers' (Table 2.3) provides an initial screening for any difficulties with the child's visual input. An affirmative answer to any of the questions means the child may have difficulties with visual input.

Implications for teachers
- If a child has visual input difficulties, a discussion should be held with the parents and the SENCO to develop an understanding of what the issues might be and how to move forward.
- Many children have glasses to overcome or minimise the effects of these types of visual difficulties. These need to be clean and need to be worn by the child.

Visual Input: Checklist for teachers

Please complete each section (tick boxes as appropriate)

	Yes	No
Does the child wear glasses?		

Child's concerns	Yes	No
Headaches		
Difficulties seeing things at a distance		
Blurred vision when reading or looking at books		
Seeing double		

Appearance of eyes	Yes	No
One eye turned in or out		
Involuntary eye movement		
Squints or screws up eyes		
Red eyes or lids; crusting on lids		

Behaviour	Yes	No
Holds book/toys close to face		
Tilts head excessively to one side or up and down		
Makes excessive head movements		
Squints or frowns to see at a distance		
Thrusts head forward to see at a distance		
Rubs eyes frequently		

Curriculum	Yes	No
Loses place when reading or skips line		
Omits words or makes errors when reading or copying		

Table 2.3   Visual input: checklist for teachers (adapted from Mandell and Fiscus 1981)

- Regardless of the type of visual problem, children can be taught to use the vision they have effectively.
- Advice and support about educational strategies and materials should be

sought from the LEA's visually impaired service, the RNIB and other specialist voluntary organisations.

Processing visual information

In addition to these visual input problems, children with physical difficulties may also have difficulties processing visual information. Disorders of visual processing are difficult to categorise (Dutton *et al.* 1999). Teachers and parents need to work together to pinpoint exactly what the difficulties are. A model which divides difficulties into place, movement, person and materials is one helpful way of representing the variety of difficulties (see Table 2.4).

Visual Processing: Checklist for teachers

Please complete each section (tick boxes as appropriate)

Area	Recognised by	Yes	No
Place			
Simultaneous perception and analysis	Finds complex visual scenes hard to recognise, for example: • difficulty finding toy on a patterned carpet • can read short words but difficulty with long words		
Depth analysis	• appears clumsy • difficulties in distinguishing between a line on the floor and a step		
Movement			
Moving past objects	• appears disorientated in school • cannot find objects in classroom		
Movement of objects	• has difficulty tracking objects • prefers TV programmes with limited movement		
Person			
Recognition of people/faces	• can see distant object but does not recognise people even when nearby		
Materials			
Spatial orientation	• difficulties with jigsaws and abstract puzzles • difficulties with copying – especially off a board • difficulties learning how to read		
Visual memory	• difficulties holding visual images in head apparent when drawing and copying		

Table 2.4   Visual processing: checklist for teachers

Implications for teachers

- Children may have perfect sight and may not need glasses, but may still have difficulties processing information visually.
- They require advice from the visually impaired service within the LEA and specialist assessment, arranged by the local paediatrician.
- They may require modifications to the school and classroom, e.g. colour coding on doors, classrooms organised, and use of language to guide the child around the school.
- They may require modifications to how visual material is presented to prevent becoming flooded, e.g. material enlarged and simplified, plain backgrounds used.
- They may require modifications of teaching style, e.g. presentation of material verbally rather than in written form, complex information presented sequentially, reduction of need to copy off a board.
- They may have difficulties with visual attention.
- They also tire more easily with new materials or in a new situation.
- They need extra time to just look at visual materials in order to make sense of them.
- Improvement can be seen in children with these types of visual processing difficulties with early intervention programmes.

Hearing

Some children with physical disabilities have hearing difficulties. The child's hearing can be affected in only one ear (unilateral) or both ears (bilateral). As hearing is central to all communication, the age of onset of a hearing problem is very significant. If the child has been born with a hearing loss (a congenital hearing loss) or if it occurs before the child is approximately 3 years old then there are major implications for the development of language. This is known as a prelingual hearing loss. The danger is that a child with severe physical difficulties and a hearing loss may be wrongly thought of as having severe learning difficulties and his hearing difficulties may not be recognised.

If children develop hearing difficulties after the age of 3, after language has developed, their difficulties are very different. This is known as a postlingual hearing loss. They are likely to be able to understand speech even if the quality of their own speech is affected.

Hearing is usually measured along two dimensions:

loudness is measured in decibels (dB); it is concerned with how loud the sound must be for the child to hear it;

frequency is measured in hertz (Hz).

It is concerned with which pitches of sound, in terms of high and low frequency, the child can hear.

The child's hearing loss is described as how loud a sound has to be at each frequency for him to hear. This is usually subdivided into a level of loss:

- mild loss (25–40 dB) – has difficulty with distant sounds or speech in a noisy environment;
- moderate loss (41–55 dB) – has difficulty understanding speech;
- severe loss (56–80 dB) – can only understand speech using a hearing aid (i.e. the sound is amplified); and
- profound loss (81 dB and above) – cannot understand speech even using a hearing aid.

Completing the 'Hearing: Checklist for teachers' provides an initial screening for any hearing difficulties.

A negative answer to any of the questions in Table 2.5 means the child may have a hearing difficulty.

Types of hearing loss
A distinction can be made between two sorts of hearing loss:

- conductive; and
- sensorineural.

Hearing: Checklist for teachers

Please complete each section (tick boxes as appropriate)

	Yes	No
Does the child have a hearing aid?		

Child's reactions	Yes	No
Reacts to loud noises		
Turns to sounds		
Reacts to speech by vocalisation		
Understands speech at an age-appropriate level		

Behaviour	Yes	No
Seems interested in the world		
Understands questions		
Plays with other children		
Reacts appropriately to requests		

Table 2.5 Hearing: checklist for teachers

These two types can sometimes be mixed. A conductive hearing loss occurs when there is interference in the conduction of sound waves through the outer and middle ear to the inner ear. This interference may be due to an infection, a foreign substance or a build-up of wax. A conductive impairment causes an even loss of hearing across all frequencies. A conductive hearing loss can often be treated. However, it may re-occur, and the child needs to be screened by regular hearing tests to monitor his hearing. The child may require a hearing aid.

A sensorineural hearing loss occurs when the inner ear or the nerves to the brain do not work properly. There is likely to be variable loss at different frequencies. In other words the child may be able to hear some frequencies at normal volume and others need to be very loud to be heard. Sensorineural loss cannot be treated by surgery; the child is likely to require a hearing aid. A hearing aid, however, simply boosts the volume of the sound. It cannot enhance clarity. The child may therefore be able to hear and react to sounds but may not be able to understand speech.

Hearing aids

Hearing aids amplify sound, that is make it louder. They are not able to replace sounds that the child can't hear. The earphone of the hearing aid is attached to an ear mould and the aid itself can be in a pocket or a harness on the body. Most aids can be used with loop wiring. This allows the teacher to use a radio transmission system to speak directly to the child, thus eliminating background noise from the classroom. Some hearing aids can magnify sound at only selected frequencies, which is extremely helpful for children with a selected hearing loss.

Hearing aids can be particularly difficult for children with physical difficulties if they do not have the fine motor movements to adjust them themselves.

Implications for teachers

- If a child has hearing difficulties a discussion should be held with the parents and SENCO to develop an understanding of what the issues might be and how to move forward.
- The child should sit at the front of the class so that he can lip-read.
- Use visual cues and aids whenever possible.
- The teacher should understand how any hearing aid works and should be able to check that it is functioning properly.
- Advice and support about educational strategies and materials should be sought from the LEA's hearing impaired service.
- Advice and support about communication should be sought from a speech and language therapist who specialises in hearing-impaired children, the RNID and other specialist voluntary organisations.

Epilepsy

Epilepsy is an umbrella term used to describe children who have fits. Fits, or seizures as they are sometimes called, are caused by changes in neurological activity in the brain. The fit can be seen as a change in muscle tone, loss of awareness or mental flashes or images. The fit may also cause convulsions, where the child's muscles involuntarily contract. Convulsions are apparent if the child stiffens, followed by some jerky movements.

Epilepsy is associated with the brain and therefore there is increased likelihood that children whose physical difficulties also stem from difficulties in the brain are likely to have epilepsy. In particular, many children with quadraplegic cerebral palsy also have epilepsy. About a third of the children with spina bifida and hydro-cephalus have convulsions (Hall and Hill 1996). Most types of epilepsy are treated with drugs. There are many different types of drug programmes, but most have side-effects. In particular, the child's attention and motivation may be affected.

Implications for teachers
- There should be written information from the child's paediatrician about what to do if there is a seizure. This should include details of the drug programme and any parts of the curriculum that the child should not take part in (e.g. swimming).
- Some common drugs require intrusive procedures (e.g. rectal diazepam) and require the school to have agreed procedures for their administration.
- Consult the DfEE guidelines for schools on supporting pupils with medical needs (DfEE 1996).
- All drugs have side-effects and the teacher is in a very good position to notice changes in mood, motivation and behaviour which should be discussed with the parents and the SENCO.
- Changes in the seizure pattern or type should also be monitored as they may indicate the child is unwell, stressed or bored.
- Epilepsy may affect educational progress through the seizures themselves (loss of memory), the effects of the drugs (drowsiness) or through lowering teacher expectation of what can be achieved.

In addition to these three secondary difficulties, children with physical difficulties may have communication problems which require an Alternative or Augmentative Communication system (AAC). This is dealt with in Chapter 5.

Visual	Yes	No	Don't know	Equipment used/ required	Comments
Visual input					
Visual processing					
Auditory	**Yes**	**No**	**Don't know**	**Equipment used/ required**	**Comments**
Conductive					
Sensorineural					
Medical	**Yes**	**No**	**Don't know**	**Equipment used/ required**	**Comments**
Epilepsy					
Other (specify)					

Table 2.6   Summary of secondary difficulties

The management of physical difficulties

Knowing the child's medical conditions, for example cerebral palsy, gives an initial starting point for understanding the child's physical difficulties. Identifying any secondary difficulties helps to plan for his education. However, there are often not easy ways to overcome these difficulties. It is important to recognise both the similarities and the differences between children with physical difficulties. A teacher will have a basic framework for the teaching of reading to a 7-year-old and then particular strategies for individual children. In the same way there are general basic frameworks for the physical management of children in the classroom and individual strategies for particular children. It is usually the physiotherapists (and the occupational therapist), in consultation with the parents and teachers, who decide on this framework and the particular strategies for the individual child. Teachers' knowledge of how the child physically manages in school is vital to setting up this programme of physical management.

There are two sorts of barriers to the child achieving full physical independence. One sort is the difficulty the child has in moving his body; the other sort are things in the environment that limit the child's ability to use the physical skills he has. So one child may have difficulty walking, but may still be able to move independently into the hall at lunchtime with a powered wheelchair. Another child with identical physical difficulties may not have this same degree of independent functioning. This can be for a number of reasons:

- he does not have a powered wheelchair;
- he has a powered wheelchair but there is not a ramp into the hall;
- he has a powered wheelchair but is not encouraged to use it; or
- he has a powered wheelchair but the battery is flat.

The management of the child's physical difficulties must then not only address the actual difficulties but also how the environment around the child is being managed. It is the failure to address the environmental constraints that turns a difficulty into a disability.

Types of physical management programmes to address the child's physical difficulties

In the same way that there are different beliefs about the most effective way of teaching reading, there are also different beliefs about the most effective way of addressing the child's physical difficulties. In this country the two most common approaches are Bobarth and Conductive Education. These approaches are designed to provide an individual physical management programme that takes into account the age of the child, the severity of his physical difficulties and his motivation.

Bobarth
Karl and Berta Bobarth developed the Bobarth programme in England in the 1940s. In the Bobarth programme the child is given specialised handling that aims to reduce stiffness, help increase muscle control against gravity and stabilise fluctuating muscle activity (Scope 1995). There are three phases of treatment:

- giving the child the sensation of what normal tone and movement feels like;
- helping the child to initiate movements during purposeful activity with the therapists' help; and
- encouraging the child to practise normal movements with a minimum of control by the therapist.

Many physiotherapists working with children (paediatric physiotherapists) are Bobarth-trained. Bobarth therapy requires physiotherapists to give the child 'hands on' therapy on a regular basis. In addition, the child will require help with a programme of exercises in the school.

Conductive education
Conductive education was developed in Hungary by Andras Peto at the end of the Second World War. It caused considerable interest when introduced to this country in the 1980s. In Hungary conductive education was developed in a

residential setting where the role of teacher and the therapists was taken on by a single person known as a conductor. She was responsibile for all the child's learning and development. In this country there are a number of models of conductive education, ranging from residential schools to units in mainstream schools, through to preschool 'Schools for Parents'. Unlike Bobarth, conductive education is not built on an analysis of the difficulties of specific muscles. Instead, children are encouraged to develop their own best ways for functional movement – known as orthofunction. This can be contrasted with Bobarth, where the child is encouraged to develop normal patterns of movement.

Children are encouraged to work to keep their position, often through the use of slatted plinths or a ladder-backed chair, which give the child something to grip on to. 'Rhythmic intention' is used where the child says what he is going to do and then counts the movement through. For example, 'I pick up my pencil – 1...2...3...4...5'. This self-talk is seen to reinforce the physical functioning. Some physiotherapists use aspects of conductive education in their physical management programmes.

Evidence of the effectiveness of the different approaches
Both of these approaches have their loyal adherents who believe that their methods are the most effective ways of helping children develop physical skills. Like many other areas of education and development there is limited research evidence to conclude which approach is best. No study has been done that shows conclusively that one particular type of intervention is more successful than others.

Work on evaluating the Bobarth type of programme has highlighted the difficulties of measuring effectiveness when there are different goals for different interventions (Bower and McLellan 1994). So a principle difficulty in evaluating effectiveness is whether the goals are about changes in patterns of movements or in functional skills.

The most rigorous research on conductive education was carried out by Bairstow *et al.* (1993). They concluded that children using conductive education made no more progress in either motor skills or learning than children in a control group who were having Bobarth physiotherapy.

It is reasonable to assume that the parents, therapists, teachers and, most importantly, the child's attitude to a particular treatment are the major determinants of its success. This does not simply mean that belief in a particular type of intervention makes it successful. Rather, it is an acknowledgement that different professionals have different skills, often gained over years of practice. In addition, different parents have different lifestyles and values, and finally, different children react differently to similar physical management programmes. What is important is to integrate the physical management programme into the school day. One way of doing this is through an American programme called MOVE.

MOVE (Mobility Opportunities Via Education)

MOVE was developed by Linda Didabe in the USA in the 1990s. Unlike the other two programmes for physical management described above, this one was devised directly for use in schools. MOVE is described as an activity-based curriculum designed to teach children basic, functional motor skills (MOVE 1995). The skills that the child and family wish to achieve are first identified (as opposed to identifying the child's physical difficulties). The focus for these are the movement skills that the child requires to function within the community. The teaching programme then uses the pupil's highest levels of ability in order to find a way to achieve these physical skills.

The MOVE curriculum breaks essential skills into 16 categories. The most important ones are:

- maintaining a sitting position;
- movement while sitting;
- standing;
- transition from sitting to standing;
- transition from standing to sitting; and
- walking forward.

These categories are then divided, into four levels of success. The levels of success are closely tied to the amount of adult help the child will require for his mobility. So the top – 'Grad Level' – assures independent mobility in the home and minimal assistance in the community. The second highest level (Level 1) assures that no lifting of the child will be required. How these skills are taught is based on the physiotherapist developing the individual child's programme. This can be based on a Bobarth or conductive education analysis. However, instead of the physiotherapist undertaking the individual direct programme himself, he trains the teacher and teaching assistant to actually deliver the programme as part of the school curriculum. MOVE very directly involves teachers in addressing the physical difficulties of the child.

Ensuring the school and classroom are accessible as part of the physical management programme

As well as being involved in addressing the child's physical difficulties the teacher is also central in ensuring the school and the classroom are accessible. It is important to know the child's functional skills before he starts in a class. This allows for planning for any classroom adaptations that are required. If this is the first year in the school it is also necessary to plan for any school adaptations that are required. This needs to be tied to the school's Access Plan under the Special Educational Needs and Disability Act 2001 (see Chapter 8 for more details). The resources for these adaptations come from central government through the Schools Access Initiative. This funding is given by the DfES, through the LEA, to schools. All nursery, primary and secondary schools are eligible for support. Schools have to submit an application to the LEA detailing the resources that are required to make the school accessible. These resources do not have to be tied to a particular child with a physical disability. However, it strengthens the urgency of the request if it includes an analysis of the functional physical skills of a child who is about to start at the school.

The Schools Access Initiative gives criteria for the allocation of resources. These are improvements to:

- **physical access to the school** – including setting down and picking up points, ramps, handrails and lifts and improvement to escape provisions;
- **physical movement around the school** – including ramps, handrails and lifts to ensure access to classrooms as well as to social areas such as the dining room and school hall;
- **access to the National Curriculum** – including specialist furniture such as desks, rise and fall tables, sinks and oven; it also includes information technology equipment (both hardware and software);
- **accommodation within the school** – including toilet facilities and developing medical rooms.

In addition, resources can be applied for to enhance the continuation of access across primary and secondary education and to reduce the travel time for pupils with a physical disability to get to school.

An analysis of what improvements would be most helpful to ensure access is best done in a collaborative way with all those involved. If adaptations are being done with one particular child in mind, it certainly helps to have the involvement of both the parents and the child. This gives a very clear message both of support and of their role in the effective inclusion. There may well be specialist support teachers in the LEA who have a particular brief in this area. In addition, both physiotherapists and, in particular, occupational therapists have particular training and expertise in this area. Involving them in the planning process is helpful, ensuring a shared vision of how the school can be adapted.

Table 2.7 provides a format for analysis of adaptations and equipment required.

Summary

Physical disability is an umbrella term that covers a whole range of physical difficulties.

- These physical difficulties stem from a range of medical conditions.
- The child may have secondary problems including visual and hearing difficulties and epilepsy.
- The child may be disabled by these difficulties if he does not have appropriate support, equipment and school and classroom adaptations.
- The physical management programme is focused on overcoming two types of barriers: (a) the child's physical difficulties, (b) the environment which hinders the child using his skills.
- The teacher and TA have a direct role in addressing the child's physical difficulties.
- The school needs to use the government's Access Initiative to develop the school and classroom environment.

1. What school adaptations are required?

	School adaptation required	Equipment required
Arrival at school		
Transition between lessons		
Breaks		
Toileting		
Mealtimes		
End of school		
Other (specify)		

2. What classroom adaptations are required?

	School adaptation required	Equipment required
Positioning e.g. sitting/standing frame		
Position in class (e.g. lighting)		
Transition between activities		
Whole-class teaching		
Small-group teaching		
Individual teaching		
Other (please specify)		

Table 2.7 School and classroom adaptations

CHAPTER 3

Working with Parents

The lives of parents

The new Code of Practice (DfES 2001a) recognises that parents' support for inclusion is vital to its success. Parents of children with physical difficulties may be very pro-inclusion and want their child in the mainstream school, or they may be quite antagonistic, feeling that their child would be better educated in a special school or unit. There may be ambiguity for many parents in their position. For example, parents of children with physical disabilities may support inclusion but not think that it is right for their own child. Teachers should not make the automatic assumption that parents would inevitably want inclusion if only there were sufficient resources; many do not (Jenkinson 1997, 1998). This chapter examines parents' concerns about inclusion and suggests strategies for building a cooperative working arrangement between them and the school.

Parents' concerns about professionals

Many parents do not believe that professionals understand what it is like to bring up a child with physical difficulties (Beresford 1995). Parents therefore often feel isolated and distanced from professionals. There are a number of reasons for this (adapted from Beresford 1995 and Darling 1993):

The child as the problem: Parents don't like the way professionals usually focus on their child as having the problem. Most professionals work, whether they be teachers or physiotherapists, on changing the child – helping the child to develop. Parents feel that many of the problems their children face are to do with constraints and difficulties outside the child. So, for example, parents may think that the problems of toileting are more to do with the fact that there are no adapted toilets in the school, or the absence of TA support for toileting, rather than the child's physical difficulties.

Expertise: Parents believe that there is an unwillingness to acknowledge that they are the experts on their own children. Parents believe that they know a great deal about their own children, which is largely unknown to teachers (Wolfendale 1992). This includes:

- their early development before they started school;
- the differences between their behaviour and functioning at school and home;
- their child's reactions to previous learning experiences; and
- their child's moods and feelings.

In the box: Parents see professionals working in a context. That context may be a Child Development Centre or, for teachers, a school within an LEA. Parents believe that professionals' views on their child are shaped by the context in which the teacher is working – professionals find it difficult to think (or see) 'outside the box'. In particular, parents are concerned about how resources seem to be allocated in a bureaucratic way. This may often be done on the basis of a formula imposed by the LEA. This will place the child in a certain category and then support will be allocated on that basis. Such a system may be defended on grounds of equality but many parents see it as unfair as it does not take into account the individual needs of their child.

A single focus: Parents are concerned that professionals are only interested in one aspect of their child. So speech and language therapists are only concerned with speech and language, doctors are only concerned with their medical health and teachers are only concerned about progress on the National Curriculum. Each professional sees the child from their own particular viewpoint. For parents this does not make sense, concerned as they are with the whole child.

Changes in professionals: Finally, parents find it difficult to deal with the changes of professionals. Teachers usually only last a year before the child moves class. Other professionals will be seen less frequently, and then, in a couple of years, may leave the area entirely. These changes in staff make it difficult, in a practical way, for the parents who have to constantly explain and re-explain their child's difficulties and progress. The transitory nature of professionals also affects parents at a psychological level. Starting school is an important and difficult transition point in these children's lives. The difficulty for the family is that the child is seen as borrowed by the school. However, there is a recognition that, both literally and metaphorically, at the end of the day the child will come home. It will be once again the parents' responsibility to look after the child and to help him along life's path. The parents, therefore, see the teacher not only as someone who can help their child along this path, but also ultimately as someone who is not responsible if the child becomes stranded half-way along. Many parents feel that only they can shoulder that responsibility. However, the knowledge that the teacher will do her best for their child is of immense support for all parents.

General issues for parents bringing up a child with physical difficulties

Children with physical difficulties are not a homogeneous group. They have diverse physical abilities and diverse educational needs. Despite these differences, these parents face many similar experiences. They have to make emotional sense of an unexpected event in their lives – giving birth to a child with a physical difficulty. This is shaped by how others (professionals and relatives) react to this event, the practical resources of the family and the type and severity of the disability (Darling 1993). However, as well as making sense emotionally of events, there are also practical issues. Children with physical difficulties make demands over and above ordinary parenting (Beresford 1995). These demands are in terms of time, money, housing and expertise.

Time: It has been estimated that the parents of a young child with severe physical difficulties have to spend over 40 hours a week simply dealing with their basic needs. This includes such things as preparing food in a special way, feeding and turning the child at night.

Money: Families of children with a disabled child have lower income than equivalent families. This is because parents' employment is affected. It can be affected by one of the parents not being able to work, given the time issues outlined above. In addition, the main wage earner may not be able to seek promotion within the normal job market. Finally, there are extra financial costs involved in bringing up a child with a physical disability; for example, extra laundry, heating or adaptations to the home.

Housing: Many families of children with physical disabilities are living in unsuitable housing. It is unsuitable not because it is worse than other housing but because of the additional needs of the child. Some of these needs relate to space – for example for wheelchairs – some relates to access – particularly to upstairs level. It may not be a problem when the child is 3 or 4, but when they become 7 and 8 it becomes increasingly difficult or impossible to use the upstairs of a house that has not been specifically adapted. And, of course, if money is short, then there are difficulties with conversions.

Expertise: When a child with a physical difficulty is born into a family the parents have to make sense of this new event in their lives. However, at a practical level they also have to develop a whole range of new skills. These may range from administering medication, through preparing special meals to undertaking a programme of physical management. Each of these requires the parents to learn new skills. An additional problem is that sometimes there is no simple solution to a child's difficulties. In other words the parents have to try out different drug regimes or eating programmes, as there is no clear indication what may be most successful.

Teachers will recognise all the above issues. They mirror the issues that teachers have to face when a child with a physical difficulty is included in the school. In the teacher's case it is also the extra time required for teaching; resources, in terms of equipment in the classroom; adaptations to the school; and finally, the new skills required to understand and manage successfully the child's physical difficulties. In a similar way to the parents, teachers also face the dilemma of not knowing what way of teaching this child will be most successful. Recognising the parallel issues for parents and teachers provides a basis for a bond of understanding.

Developing independence skills

As children go through nursery and infant schools they develop greater independence. This is part of the whole process of growing up. Teachers have a key role in many parts of this process of developing independence, from helping children to learn to dress, to using a knife and fork. Children with physical difficulties may have particular problems in these areas (see Figure 3.1). The difficulties that children with physical difficulties have in developing independence skills have both an emotional and a practical impact.

Mealtimes can cause particular distress. It is very difficult for parents to have a young child that has difficulties feeding, one of the basic human instincts. At a practical level some difficulties with feeding can mean that mealtimes often have to take hours each day. In addition, feeding difficulties can be due to difficulties with muscles in the mouth which can make swallowing problematic and even dangerous. Feeding difficulties can also mean concern about weight gain and the need for dietary advice and support. There are, in addition, a very small number of children with physical difficulties who need to be fed through a 'peg' in their stomach. Though this in itself is a minor surgical intervention, it can often be seen as a significant difficulty.

Toileting can also be a significant difficulty for many children with physical difficulties. Once again, the difficulties can be largely practical in terms of accessibility. For some children their physical condition means that it is highly unlikely that they will ever gain bladder or bowel control. This, again, has a practical and psychological impact on their families.

The difficulties with independence skills may not be too onerous in themselves,

Independence Skills: Checklist for teachers

Please complete each section (tick boxes as appropriate)

Areas of independence

Dressing	Tick one
Can dress self at an age-appropriate level	
Can dress self when clothes are laid out	
Can help to dress self with some physical help	
Totally dependent for dressing	

Undressing	Tick one
Can undress self at an age-appropriate level	
Can undress self with some physical help	
Can help to undress self with considerable physical help	
Totally dependent for undressing	

Mealtimes	Tick one
Can feed self independently at an age-appropriate level	
Can feed self with spoon if food is cut	
Can help feed self but spoon needs loading	
Totally dependent for feeding	
Has difficulties swallowing (food or drink)	
Needs all foods to be liquidised	
Has special dietary requirements	
Has specialised feeding arrangements (e.g. 'peg feed')	

Toileting	Tick one
Can use toilet at an age-appropriate level	
Needs help accessing toilet but can then manage own needs	
Needs help accessing toilet and with toileting needs	
Bowel though not bladder control	
No bowel or bladder control	

Table 3.1   Independence skills: checklist for teachers

but put together with the general issues outlined above, they can become very stressful. All children are, initially, totally dependent. However, for many parents of children with physical difficulties it is the long-term aspect of care and dependency that is so tiring.

The areas of difficulty with skills of independent living are listed in Table 3.1 and summarised in Table 3.2:

Sub-area	Yes	No	Don't know	Equipment used/required	Comments
Dressing					
Undressing					
Mealtimes					
Toileting					

Table 3.2 Summary of independence difficulties

The parents' search for normalisation

Bringing up a child with physical difficulties can be highly stressful. Parents are at high risk of psychological stress – significantly higher than parents of children with other types of special educational needs, for example children with Down's syndrome or severe learning difficulties (Sloper and Turner 1991, 1993). However, although it is important to recognise the difficulties in bringing up a child with a physical disability, it is equally important to acknowledge how well some families adapt (Byrne and Cunningham 1985).

Parents can be seen as looking for 'normalisation' of their life in the light of the needs of their child. Families are looking for services which will allow them to live the life they were expecting, before the birth of their child – the same sort of lifestyle as the families of non-disabled children. This desire to adapt, or normalise, their lives is a major motivating force for families (Seligman and Darling 1989).

Opportunity structures

Certain 'opportunity structures' are required if normalisation is to occur. Such opportunity structures can be material, practical or psychological. For example, having a car can significantly help a family, as can guidance on mealtimes, as can emotional support from a grandparent. All the opportunity structures listed below can help parents in their search for normalisation:

- access to satisfactory medical advice and care through the GP;
- supportive relatives and friends;
- presence of accepting neighbours;
- presence of friends and social opportunities for the child;
- access to respite care and day care if needed;
- adequacy of financial resources;
- quantity and quality of household help;
- availability of appropriate leisure activities;
- access to special equipment, if needed;
- adequacy of available transport; and
- availability of appropriate schooling.

In terms of appropriate education, opportunity structures are not confined to the local mainstream school. The paradox is that a family may believe that normalisation for their child (and family) can best happen if the child is at a special school or unit. How a family decides whether appropriate schooling is mainstream or special is returned to later in the chapter.

These opportunities may change, for example, if a family moves, if they meet helpful professionals, or if there is promotion at work. In other words a family's ability to normalise must be seen within the context of their life in a community. Opportunity structures may also change at points of 'transition'. One of the main transition points is starting school. There are smaller transition points in school – for example changing class or having a new teacher. Transition points also occur in the family's life. If a parent becomes chronically ill, a support person (a grandparent) dies or leaves, or if someone is made redundant, then the family is increasingly vulnerable. At these transition points the support and stability of the school is particularly important.

Mainstream school can clearly be an opportunity structure that helps the normalisation of the child and family. To work in this way, placement in mainstream has to remove stress from these parents, not increase their already stressed and pressured lives. Alternately, if the mainstream placement means the parents have to attend additional appointments after school, cope with erratic transport arrangements and fight for school adaptations, they may well believe that they would achieve a more normal life if their child went to a special school where all these difficulties were dealt with easily.

Making inclusion an opportunity for normalisation

There are a range of options for parents of children with physical difficulties before they start school. Some children will stay at home, some will attend an ordinary playgroup or nursery and some will go to a special nursery or unit attached to a special school or child development centre. Parents' experiences of these provisions shape their attitude to their child starting mainstream school.

If children attend an ordinary playgroup or nursery it is likely that their parents will believe that inclusion benefits development. However, parents of children who are in special preschool provision may well be less positive about inclusion and think that children in a mainstream school have a lower quality of education (Bailey and Winton 1987).

There is a link between preschool provision and the future school placement. Children who attend preschool special provision are much more likely to attend special school than those who attend preschool mainstream provision. Vice versa, children who attend preschool mainstream provision are much more likely to go on to a mainstream school. This process goes on, it seems, informally alongside the formal assessment for a Statement. The majority of parents of preschool children with physical difficulties decide on their child's schooling before the completion of the Statementing process.

The government recognises that parents need to be involved in the decision for their child to go to mainstream school. Parents' satisfaction with mainstream depends more on them being involved in the decision than on the actual severity of the child's physical difficulty or the amount of physiotherapy he receives. It is therefore vital that parents are listened to when they initially come to the local mainstream school to discuss the possibility of inclusion. These conversations are likely to be led by the head teacher. However, both the SENCO and the child's potential class teacher should also be involved. It is also worth involving other agencies at this initial stage. Many parents find inter-agency working poor and it can become a major stressor for many families. To start the inclusion process by working in a coordinated and cooperative way with other agencies is a particularly strong message for parents. In particular, consideration should be given to how the physiotherapy service can be involved. Parents have a range of concerns about their child coming to a mainstream school (Fox 1999). These are areas that have the potential to cause parents stress. By being aware of these areas teachers can not only reassure parents but also put practical strategies into place to deal with the issues.

Parent's concerns about inclusion

Relationships
Many parents are concerned that their child will have good relationships with their peers and be accepted into the class. They want them to have friends to sit near and children to play with. Many parents worry that this is not going to happen and that, instead, their child will be teased or even bullied. Support from a sibling or close relative already at the school is one key strategy. If this is not possible, it is helpful to identify children who live in the same street as a point of contact for new

parents. In addition, there is a range of strategies that schools can use to facilitate the development of friendships both in the classroom and at breaktime (see Chapter 6).

Education

Despite, or because of, their physical difficulties, many parents are concerned about their child's progress on the National Curriculum. They are aware that it is their child's educational progress that will ultimately decide how he will benefit from mainstream. So, initially, they want to be reassured that their child is progressing in such fundamental areas as reading and mathematics. If the child is having difficulties in a key area such as writing, they need to be reassured that attention will be given to solving this (either through practice and/or alternative means of recording his work).

Development

As well as making progress on the National Curriculum, parents are also concerned that their child is progressing in a number of developmental areas. Most importantly, this is about the development of the child's physical skills. Parents want to know how the child's physical management programme will be incorporated into the school day. There may be other areas of development, for example communication skills, which are central to the parents. Finally, there is the development of independence skills that make such a difference to parents.

School

Parents have a range of concerns about the school itself. At the most fundamental level this will include getting to the school. If it is the local mainstream school, then parents are likely to bring their child, but there may be implications for this if they have other children who also need taking to school or need looking after. Once at school, issues emerge concerning the accessibility of the school. Is the school all on one level? If not, how is the child going to get to the first floor or even up stairs? Are ramps in place for a child who uses a wheelchair? Another part of accessibility, especially for a child in a wheelchair, is the width of corridors, and especially doors.

Safety

The fact that the child has physical difficulties means that parents are concerned that he will be safe. Even a slight concern in this area will override all the other positive features of a mainstream school. Feeling safe is about addressing the child's physical vulnerability in unstructured situations such as the playground. Many parents are concerned that their child may be pushed or may fall accidentally. Some children may have secondary problems such as epilepsy or swallowing difficulties. These require clear guidelines in place, including the administration of drugs. Parents will need to be reassured that school can deal with any emergency for these specific conditions.

General

As well as all these specific areas, parents will have concerns that can best be described as 'free floating'. Parents want their child to be happy, to be loved and to have a chance in life. Addressing this is to do with the culture of the school and the attitude of the head teacher and staff being positive and welcoming. The attitudes of the teachers are really important in terms of warmth, sensitivity and acceptance of the child.

Parents' concerns about the relationship between their child and their peers, and their safety, often diminish once school starts. However, in other areas parents' concerns do not change once their children are in school. Parents carry the concerns they have before their children start school through to when the child is in school. So parents' concerns in the above areas may persist even though there are no particular problems in the school. For example, parents may continue to be concerned that their child is making progress with his reading even when there are no difficulties in this area. Teachers need to recognise that these are just natural anxieties by parents and not criticisms of the school.

Understanding parents' perceptions

Models of disability

Two contrasting models help explain how parents, and professionals, view disability (Quinn 1998). They are known as the:

- individual (or medical) model of disability; and the
- social model of disability.

Individual (or medical) model of disability

The individual model of disability is largely based on a belief that the individual child is disabled because of their medical condition (cerebral palsy, spina bifida). Medical conditions require treatment, and in this way the child can overcome his disability. As long as the child, and his family, follow the professionals' advice, and their suggested treatment, they will get better. There are clearly implications for how families are viewed who do not follow the treatment programme, and who do not get better.

Special education legislation in Britain is based on an individual model of disability. The individual model is, as is all of education, a developmental model where the focus of education is for the child to learn new skills. Effective education is defined as how much progress children can make to overcome their difficulties. Special educational needs are defined as deviance from the norm and the Annual Review and Individual Educational Plans (IEPs) measure progress towards new attainments. Parents who hold an individual model of disability will want to see their child progressing by developing new skills. They will want 'programmes', 'treatment' and 'education' to overcome their child's disability and to help him to develop.

Social model of disability

In contrast, the 'social' model of disability is based on the view that, though a child with a physical difficulty may not have the same physical skills as his peers, the problems he encounters are largely due to what happens around him. In other words, it is the social context that he lives in that causes the problems. These problems may be to do with other people, such as negative attitudes or prejudice, or may be due to the environment, such as access to, and within, schools. For adults with a physical difficulty the problems are seen to be about the inaccessibility of many public buildings, the difficulties with transport and the whole economic system that makes it difficult for them to earn a good wage. The social disability model sees the problems as that of society – not as that of the child with a disability (Swain et al. 1993). Parents who hold a social view of disability do not see the priority as treatment, or programmes to overcome their child's physical difficulty. Rather, they see the priority in the positive attitudes of staff, good relationships with peers, appropriate equipment and adaptations to schools which ensure their children are included in the real world.

Dimensions of inclusion

Parents can, therefore, focus on two dimensions to achieve a normal family life:

- their child's development; and
- their child's inclusion in the real world.

They may think that their child's development is the priority, and that if only he could overcome his physical difficulty then life would be normal. Or they may believe that if only society (and school) would be more accepting of their child's difficulties then life would be normal. Of course, they may also think that both are true. The two dimensions are represented in Figure 3.1 as two scales, with 10 representing a high level of focus and 1 a low focus, on each particular dimension.

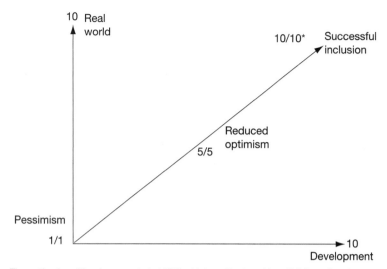

The optimal position for parents is 10/10 – high on Real world and high on Development

Figure 3.1   Dimensions of inclusion

In education these two dimensions can be pulling in different directions. Parents who want inclusion focus in the direction of the real world. Parents who want special schools focus in the direction of development. However, effective inclusion means that they have to work together.

Parents can take up a variety of positions on the diagram, which are summarised below.

10/10 – Successful inclusion: high on Development/high on Real world
Parents who take this position believe that it is important to focus on both areas. They believe strongly in inclusion and the development of their children. This is only possible if they believe that the mainstream school has the attitude, knowledge, skills and resources to ensure optimum development for their child.

10/1 – Real world focus: high on Real world/low on Development
A real world focus is tied to an inclusive view of the world and a belief that inclusion in mainstream school is the priority. Parents who take this position strongly believe in the importance of their child being in the real world. Their concerns about development may be low because of particular support they receive in their community or because the development of skills is not a priority for them.

1/10 – Developmental focus: high on Development/low on Real world
Parents who take this position believe that the development of their child's skills is of prime importance. They believe that the development of skills is the main focus

of education. Inclusion in the real world is less important to them. This may be because they believe their child has such severe difficulties that he may never be able to function in the real world. Or they may believe that education is a dynamic process and that the focus in the early years has to be on the development of skills. By focusing on the development of skills they may believe that their child will be more likely to be able to function in the real world as an adult.

5/5 – Reduced optimistic focus: medium on Development and the Real world
Parents who take this position have temporarily lost their belief that their children can ever really have a normal life. This may happen at particular times in a child's life. It might happen if parents were told that their child would not benefit from inclusion in their local infant school or if they had been advised to stop trying for independent mobility and, instead, to use a wheelchair to get around a mainstream school. In both cases, parents may feel that schooling is not going too well.

1/1 – Pessimistic focus: low on Real world and on Development
Some parents feel very helpless and hopeless about their child. They do not believe that their child can ever be normal or that he can be in the real world. They may feel depressed about the future not only for their child but also for themselves as a family. This is not necessarily tied to the severity of the difficulties their child has. A child can have rather minor physical difficulties and the parents can still feel pessimistic. It is the difference between the parents' expectations and their child's achievements that will lead to them feeling pessimistic, or not.

The two dimensions have been outlined above in terms of parents' beliefs, as this has been the focus of this chapter. However, it is important to acknowledge that they can equally be applied to how teachers (or other professionals) see children's education. Some teachers are simply concerned with the development of children's educational achievements (1/10 developmental focus). Other teachers focus mainly on inclusion (10/1 Real World focus). Teachers can also take the other positions including the pessimistic focus and believe that they cannot really develop the children's skills or help them to be in the real world.

Helping the child to start school

The Dimensions of Inclusion are a way of understanding the conflicting expectations that parents have when their child starts at a mainstream school. To reassure parents that their child is being included successfully attention must be given to his development and to his inclusion in the real world. Parents need to be reassured about:

- good peer relationships in the school – a child without siblings and isolated from his peers in the school may not feel supported;

- a positive school atmosphere – in particular, the head teacher and staff display a friendly and caring attitude;
- provision of specialist facilities and equipment;
- appropriate inter-agency support, particularly in terms of physical management;
- a focus on educational progress;
- school and classroom accessibility; and
- safety, particularly with movement around schools and back-up medical provision.

Most parents want reassurance in these areas when their child starts school. However, they may be more difficult to achieve for children with physical difficulties.

MAPS – planning together

Throughout this book there is an emphasis on working and planning together. MAPS, a system for planning with the parents and child, is particularly useful when the child starts school.

MAPS is designed to help plan and implement a programme for inclusion for children with special education needs (Forest and Lusthaus 1990, Vandercook *et al.* 1989). It is useful for all pupils with SEN – not just those with physical difficulties. MAPS is a process in which information is shared from the child's past, present and future to plan for inclusion. One of the distinct features of MAPS is that it includes the child with a physical difficulty, and his peers, in the planning process.

Involving children in planning

Children with SEN are increasingly actively involved these days in planning for their special educational needs. The Code of Practice strengthens that involvement. One of the fundamental principles of the Code is that the views of the child must be sought and taken into account when his education is being planned. It is acknowledged that these views should be seen in the light of his age and understanding. Central to this principle is a belief that children who have been involved from an early age in planning will, when older, be more empowered to make choices about their own lifestyle. Even young children at age 4 or 5 will have views about what they enjoy doing.

MAPS also suggests that the child's peers are involved. There are a number of advantages to involving the peers:

- inclusion becomes a whole-class issue;
- peers feel empowered to make a difference;
- peers will have a different way of viewing issues;
- peers may come up with different solutions to problems; and
- peers become involved in the child's progress.

Once again, how peers are involved will depend on their age and understanding. It also depends on how well they know the child. If the child has been in a settled class for a number of years the peers will know the child well.

The involvement of peers is a decision that is taken with the parents and, most importantly, the child. It should be suggested that some of the classmates might like to join a discussion to help plan for the next term, or year. There may well be issues that the parents, or child, wish to keep confidential – and this clearly is their right. However, there are many areas where the classmates' involvement and perspectives are of significant benefit to the child.

In addition to the parents, the child and his peers, those professionals who are directly involved with the child should be part of MAPS. The teacher has a central role. Depending on the size and organisation of the school, the head teacher, the SENCO and the TA may all be involved. From outside the school there should definitely be the physiotherapist, but, once again, there may be a range of other professionals as outlined in Chapter 4. One of the issues for children with physical difficulties is the range of professionals who may be involved. There is a danger that meetings either become so large as to be unwieldy or that, vice versa, key people are missing who have vital pieces of information. The Core and Secondary teams, as described in Chapter 4, all have a part to play.

The MAPS process

There are seven key questions at the heart of MAPS. Each of these is gone through in turn. This establishes a shared understanding of what the issues are for the parents and their child. It signals that they will be listened to and that there will be a collaborative working relationship between the family and the school.

Question 1: What is the child's story?
The first area to explore is the child's story in terms of his history. The parents (and the child) should probably do most of the talking. Areas that might come up are:

- Did he attend a playgroup?
- What did he most enjoy there?
- Did he have friends who have moved to this school?
- Does he have any brothers or sisters?
- When did he get his wheelchair?

The idea is to build up a picture of the key things that have happened in the child's life. Obviously, the question can be adapted for a child who is already well known to the school. In this case it would be more appropriate to ask about their story of what has happened in the last year – or since the last review. Having the child and his parents tell their stories is an important starting point. It updates all members on what is going on for this child. It allows the child and the parents to make a major contribution at the start of the meeting. It also signals that the child is the focus of the meeting and will be listened to.

Question 2: What is your dream?

This question is designed to help people think beyond the present circumstances. It is designed to create a vision for the child's future. Underpinning most planning is moving from the present position to thinking about how things could be in the future – creating a vision. The conversation should start with the child's dream and then move on from this to the parents. It may be difficult for the child and the parents to think too far ahead. Ideally, the dream should be about how they are as an adult, what they are doing and how their life is. However, it may be only possible to think about a year or two ahead with a very young child.

Question 3: What is your nightmare?

This question can be extremely difficult and there will be times when it should not be asked. However, it is also a very important question; it forces the child and his parents to think about what they do not want to happen. By articulating what they do not want to happen it becomes easier to prevent it happening. So the child might be asked, 'If you were having a really bad nightmare about school, what would it be about?' Their answer might be about being teased, being left alone at playtime, not being able to do the homework or having to sit at the front of the class all day. These responses all give very helpful insights into how the child, and the parents, sees things.

Question 4: Who is the child?

This is the first question for everyone. Once again, the child may be the starting point but then everyone in the meeting can be asked. Everyone is asked for what words come to mind when they think of the child. It is best to go around the room in order. If someone cannot think of a word, they simply pass. All the words should be written up. At the end of the process there is a long list of words that describe the child. The child can then be asked to identify the three words they think describe them best. Parents can also be asked to do the same.

Question 5: What are the child's strengths, gifts and talents?
The importance of this question is that it starts to focus on the child's strengths. All too often, meetings only focus on the child's difficulties. This way the initial focus is on the area in which the child has strengths. The starting point for this can be the answers to Question 4. Everyone can be asked to say which words on the list describe the pupil's strengths. Once again, one can start with the child and move on to his peers.

Question 6: What does the child require for inclusion?
This question does not ask about Needs and Provision, as defined by the Code of Practice; instead, it asks more simply, 'What does the child require?' What is interesting about the question is that it highlights how different people have different views on what is required. So peers may emphasise someone to sit beside in the classroom or to go to lunch with, parents may emphasise the need for support with toileting, and the teacher may feel the main requirement is what to do about the physical management programme. Once again, the group can be questioned in turn with each member contributing one thing that they think the pupil requires.

Question 7: What would the child's ideal day at school look like?
This can start with the teacher outlining what a normal day is like for the rest of the pupils in the class. In light of the requirements brought up in answer to Question 6, the meeting can then think through how these requirements can be integrated into the school day.

At the end of the meeting everyone is asked to think of one word that describes MAPS. This is a useful way of confirming the value of the meeting. It can also throw up any difficulties people may have.

MAPS is a flexible system and can be used in different ways. It is particularly useful at transition points, for example just after the child has started a new school. The MAPS meeting could take place a little into the school year after the child has begun to settle in the new classroom. This allows the teacher, TA and peers to get to know him. MAPS works well as an informal process that allows the sharing of information and views in a collaborative, open way. However, many aspects of MAPS can be incorporated into more formal planning times, for example the Annual Review or setting Individual Educational Plans (IEPs). In these situations not all of the MAPS process will be suitable – however, the general principles hold good. These are to work together with the child, parents and teachers to review where the child is now, create a vision and plan how to move forward.

MAPS has a number of purposes. It is designed to

- ensure collaboration between the school and parents;
- allow different perspectives to be shared;

- develop a shared vision about the child;
- develop a shared language between parents and professionals;
- give the child a voice;
- involve the peers in inclusion; and
- empower the child to make decisions.

Different purposes may be important at different times. With a child newly started at school it may be most important to develop a vision and ensure a collaborative approach. Later on, it may be most important to empower the child to make decisions. By recognising that there are these different purposes, teachers can ensure that MAPS meetings are productive and worthwhile.

Summary

In this chapter the issues facing parents of children with physical difficulties are explored. In particular, it is important to recognise that

- parents will see education from a different perspective to teachers;
- parents' support for inclusion is vital to its success;
- parents often feel that professionals do not understand the issues there are in bringing up a child with a physical difficulty;
- parents are faced with practical as well as emotional difficulties;
- parents are looking to normalise their family life;
- inclusion can provide the support to make that normalisation possible;
- parents may feel torn between wanting their child included in the real world and maximising their child's development; and
- involving the child, the parents and his peers is an important starting point in collaborative working.

CHAPTER 4

Collaborative Working in Teams

Why work with others?

The effective inclusion of children with physical difficulties requires a range of people to work collaboratively with the class teacher. This includes LEA officers, the head teacher, the SENCO, professionals from a range of disciplines, the teaching assistant and, of course, the parents of the child. In addition, there may be a range of other people whose contribution may appear less immediate but whose role is also vital. These may include professionals such as dieticians, rehabilitation engineers and orthoptists. They may also include non-professionals such as grandparents, siblings and neighbours. These people may not be directly involved with the school. However, their advice and support may, at times, be crucial for the effective inclusion of the child.

This chapter examines the need for these people – particularly the professionals – to work together in teams. Teams have some particular characteristics and the professionals may be involved in different kinds of teams: a core team, or a secondary team. Different professionals have different roles and different responsibilities, and the class teacher plays a central leadership role in bringing these different teams together and using professionals' particular expertise to support effective inclusion.

What is a team?

Teams can be defined as two or more people working or meeting together on a regular basis, who have a complex interdependent task, and a common goal. The task in our case is the successful inclusion of the child and the goal is to optimise his development. There are a number of implications of this definition:

- A team can consist of just two people – for example the core team of the class teacher and TA is central to the child's successful inclusion.
- The members of the team have to work (or at least meet) together. It is very difficult to have a team with someone who is never in the school.

- There has to be some sort of common culture in terms of agreeing how things are done in the school.
- A team is required when there is a complex task which can't be resolved by an individual professional.
- The members of the team are dependent on each other.
- Members of the team must believe they have some common goals for working with the child. If professionals are working towards different ends they cannot be considered a team.

Functions fulfilled by teams

Most teams have both formal and informal functions (Schein 1988). The formal function can be seen as working on a complex interdependent task; that is a task which cannot be done by one person. The task that this book addresses is the effective inclusion of the child with a physical difficulty. For this to be done effectively it requires teamwork and cooperation from a range of people. Underpinning the task of effective inclusion are a range of other formal goals. Some of the formal goals could include

- ensuring educational progress;
- maximising physical functioning;
- developing communication skills; and
- developing social and emotional independence.

For each of these goals there are a series of targets, each of which may need the input from different professionals. For example, to ensure educational progress one of the targets might be 'to improve handwriting skills'. This would then require:

- deciding on the best position for writing;
- accessing an appropriate table;
- deciding on a teaching programme for writing;
- deciding on grouping with peers;
- undertaking fine motor activities to strengthen muscles; and
- advising parents on fine motor activities.

Effective inclusion requires a range of professionals to work on these formal tasks together.

The second important function filled by teams is informal – giving people something psychological or social. This could include:

- friendship and support – 'It's good to have someone I can rely on';
- a sense of self-esteem, of doing something worthwhile – 'She does really seem to appreciate the effort I'm making';

- establishing social reality – 'It's not just me who is having difficulty under-standing this communication system!';
- reducing insecurity, anxiety and a sense of powerlessness – 'It's good to realise that others are not certain of the best way forward.'

For many teachers it is the informal support that they get from a team that helps maintain motivation and commitment when progress is slow and targets don't seem achievable.

Working in teams

Levels of working

There are three levels of working with the child:

- direct work;
- monitoring; and
- consultancy.

In **direct work**, the professional works directly with the child either individually, in a small group or with the whole class. The professional may be teaching the child a new skill or practising a skill that he has learnt previously. In **monitoring**, the professional is involved in setting goals and monitoring the progress the child makes – but she is not directly involved with teaching. In **consultancy**, the professional does not work with the child but works directly with other professionals. The consultant advises the other professionals on how to proceed.

All professionals use these different levels of working at times. So, for example, the teacher will teach the class the names of the planets (direct work), she will mark the pupils' drawings of the planets (monitoring) and finally she will advise the parents about the most helpful way to help the child with their homework (consultancy).

One of the key decisions for each professional is about what is the most effective use of time to work at different levels. The ability to move from level to level is central to effective working. It is important not to devalue professionals who work at one particular level – consultancy is important and so is direct work with the child. Careful attention to time management is crucial if professionals are to use their skills most effectively.

Multiple teams

A number of teams will be developed around a child with a physical disability. The class teacher will take a central role in coordinating much of the work of these teams. The focus is on how the professionals work together. Parents have, there-fore, been omitted from the discussion of the different teams. This is not because they are not involved, but rather that they fit in at all levels with both teams. Practicalities will dictate how they can best be involved but they need to be central to the class teacher's thinking about the membership of the teams.

- **core team** – the professionals involved daily, or very regularly, with the child. This team usually consists of the teacher and TA. They will be doing much of the direct work with the child.
- **the secondary team** – the professionals involved directly with the child on a regular basis. This team consists of the core team plus other professionals who are working in the school and supporting the child. It is likely to consist of the physiotherapist, the speech and language therapist and the occupational therapist. It will also include specialist advisory teachers, the SENCO, local paediatricians and social workers. Some of these people will be working directly with the child, but many will have a monitoring or consultancy role.

The distinction between the two teams is in many ways somewhat arbitrary. What is important is that the teacher recognises the range of people who support the child's inclusion and the need to have greater or less involvement with each of them. Who is in each team will be a matter of local circumstances. Teams should be as inclusive as possible. People who would like to contribute should be made to feel part of a team. However, with membership of the team there also comes a commitment to become involved at that level – this may mean being involved in meetings or working directly with the child. As the child develops the composition of the team may change. So initially, it may be important for the speech and language therapist to be part of the core team but after a few years this may no longer be appropriate and they will revert to being a member of the secondary team.

The core team

Roles and responsibilities

At the heart of the core team there is the class teacher and the TA.

The class teacher
The class teacher works for the school. Most primary schools are organised so that one teacher is responsible for a class of children of the same age. The number of children in the class may range from 25 to 35. The class teacher will usually organise her class in a variety of ways with some whole-class teaching, some

small-group work and some individual teaching. The class teacher has to cover the National Curriculum and, within that, specific time is allocated for literacy and numeracy. Though the above may be obvious to the class teacher it may be less obvious to a physiotherapist or parent. It is important for others to know that the time given each day to literacy is a government requirement and not something that can be ignored. The class teacher of a child with a physical difficulty has a number of additional roles:

- teaching the child;
- championing for the child;
- liaising with the parents;
- supervising and working with the TA; and
- coordinating the core and secondary teams.

The teaching assistant

There has been a considerable increase in the number of TAs employed by schools to support children with special educational needs. Many children with a physical difficulty have their inclusion supported by a TA. TAs are often based in a particular classroom or shared across two classrooms. They work in close collaboration with the class teacher and may spend considerable time working directly with the individual child, helping them gain independence and access to the curriculum.

The TA may have worked with the class teacher (or the child) in a previous year or they may not know each other. The TA may be either full- or part-time, and may have had considerable, or little, training and experience of working with children with physical difficulties. In other words, the TA may also be on a steep learning curve with the child's teacher.

Problems with core teams

The main issue for the core team is the balance of responsibilities between the TA and the class teacher. The TA has a lower position, in terms of formal status, and there is a danger that she can feel devalued. To compensate for this, the TA may try to take on all the responsibilities for ensuring that inclusion works. She may begin to develop this status by becoming the expert on the child and by knowing more about him than the teacher. She may try to ensure that the teacher is not burdened by the child. This scenario can snowball, with the TA doing most of the communication with the parents. Soon other professionals may be going to the TA for information on how the child is progressing.

The teacher can gradually become isolated, feeling that she does not know the child very well. This may eventually lead to the situation where the TA comes to see herself as championing the child while the class teacher becomes disengaged.

There is, therefore, a paradox – the better the TA is at working with the individual child the more likely it is that the teacher will find it unnecessary to engage in his inclusion. The poorer the TA, the more likely it is that the class teacher will be centrally involved in the child's inclusion.

Working together effectively

The key to resolving this issue is to ensure that the TA has a clear role that is valued. This role is about supporting the class teacher's work with the child with a physical difficulty, rather than the individual child. This does not mean that the TA does not have some individual responsibilities with the child; on the contrary, she should, otherwise there is a danger that she may feel like a 'dogsbody' in the classroom.

For this working relationship to develop there needs to be regular, collaborative meetings between the TA and the teacher. These need to be at least weekly and, ideally, some time will need to be given daily. The teacher needs to share what she intends to teach so that the TA can think about how she can support the child. In addition, the teacher needs to plan how she can be involved directly in teaching this child and how the TA can support the whole of the class. In this way the inclusion of the child with a physical difficulty becomes a whole-class process rather than the TA working with him on a one-to-one basis.

In order to start this process knowledge of three things is required:

- the child's current functional skills, including his physical, independence and communication skills;
- school adaptations already made; and
- equipment the child already has.

This background information is obtained from the child's Statement (see Chapter 7), the meetings of the secondary team and the MAPS process (see Chapter 3). This process starts with developing the last question in MAPS – 'What would the child's ideal day at school look like?' (see Table 4.1).

This time the analsysis looks at what assistance is required both around the school and inside the classroom. This should be the starting point for the core team to work together. It will be important at some stage to bring the parents and other professionals into the discussion. If the class teacher and the TA have not worked together before, they may want to have an initial planning session together before involving others. On the other hand it may be very helpful to have the parents and physiotherapist there right from the beginning.

This analysis may not be straightforward. There may be areas where no-one is quite sure what assistance is required. However, what this process does is to allow

Section 1: Assistance around school
Question: Are daily routines outside the classroom established?

Section 2: Assistance in the classroom
Question: Are daily routines in the classroom established?

	No assistance required	Description of assistance required	Who will provide it?	Is training required?	Classroom adaptation required	Equipment required
Positioning, e.g. sitting/standing frame						
Position in class (e.g. lighting)						
Transition between activities						
Whole-class teaching						
Small-group teaching						
Individual teaching						
Other (please specify)						

Table 4.1   An ideal school day

the class teacher and TA to decide collaboratively on what assistance needs to be provided for the child. If there are difficulties with any of these areas they should be discussed with the secondary team.

Though there may be differences between the assistance given in different curriculum areas these are not identified at this stage. Instead the initial focus is on establishing the assistance required for a daily working routine that can underpin the specific timetable for the child. This timetable depends on input from the secondary team and, in particular, the identification of how the programmes for physical management can be incorporated into the school day.

The secondary team

One of the key features of the secondary team is that it is multidisciplinary. This means that members of the team will come from different professions and work for different agencies. Some will be employed by the school, some by the LEA and others by the National Health Service or the local authority's Social Services.

Roles and responsibilities

There are a large number of professionals who may be involved in the secondary team. Some of these will be working with the child directly in school but not on a daily basis. Some may be working directly with the child out of school and some will offer a consultation service on the basis of their knowledge of children with physical difficulties. Not all the professionals listed below will be involved, but many will be.

Physiotherapists (health)

Paediatric (children) physiotherapists are part of a physiotherapist team probably based in a child development centre or a community service. Physiotherapy is aimed at developing and consolidating the child's physical skills. Physiotherapists usually become involved with children with physical difficulties at a very young age. They may well see the child at home or in a playgroup or nursery. For children in school, the physiotherapist will work with the teachers to develop a physical management programme that can be incorporated into the school day (see Chapter 3).

Occupational therapists (health or social services)

Occupational therapists have a variety of roles with children with physical difficulties. Though they can be involved in direct work with the child, they usually work at the consultancy level, advising on particular issues. They work closely with the physiotherapist on the development of fine hand skills, hand–eye coordination and visual-perceptual skills. They work with the speech and language therapist on feeding. Many have a particular expertise on equipment and aids to daily living, such as mobility aids and the adaptations to toilets. Occupational therapists can work for either health or social services. Those who work for social services are more likely to specialise in equipment and adaptations to aid independence. There is a national shortage of occupational therapists with some areas having virtually no service for schools.

Speech and language therapists (health or education)

Speech and language therapists specialise in the development of communication skills. This may be about the development of speech but also the use of signing systems and other communication aids (see Chapter 5). They help children access computer-linked switching systems. There are specialist centres for the assessment of complex communication problems. Speech and language therapists are also involved with children with feeding difficulties due to problems with movement of the mouth and jaw. There is a national shortage of speech and language therapists.

Most speech and language therapists work for the health service, though some LEAs also employ them.

Community paediatricians (health)

Community paediatricians are doctors who specialise in working with children. As consultants they have a key coordinating role, leading the Child Development Team and planning for the health needs of the child. The community paediatrician is rarely in schools apart from a planning meeting such as an annual review if there are special medical difficulties. It is through the paediatrician that access to other medical specialists can be made. These can include:

- **paediatric neurologists** who specialise in childhood conditions which affect the brain, e.g. cerebral palsy;
- **ophthalmologists** who check the function of the eyes and whether the messages from the eyes can be interpreted by the brain; and
- **orthoptists** who assess the movement of the eyes.

Social workers (social services)

Social workers work for local authority social services. This is usually a discrete department within the local council. They are largely concerned with supporting and advising the family. This advice can be about financial issues, such as how to claim the Disability Living Allowance. They also have access to respite care services and can assist in setting up Family Link, babysitting and other home-based respite care services. Under the Children Act (1998) social workers' key task is the welfare of children. There is often a specialist team in social services for children with a disability.

Advice workers (voluntary agencies)

There are numerous voluntary agencies that support children with physical difficulties. Some of these are large, national organisations such as Scope or Contact a Family. Many are smaller, serving a specific community. Voluntary organisations may have a number of functions. Most supply specialist information on the areas that they are interested in. Some provide support and advocacy services to the family or the child. Some will help with funds for resources and specialist equipment. The advice workers who work for voluntary agencies are not constrained by local policies and procedures. Instead, they will often have a national or regional overview in terms of what is possible. They also usually work in one specialist area, for example muscular dystrophy or cerebral palsy. This means that they know a lot about this particular area and are good at offering independent information and advice.

Problems with secondary teams

The main issue for working in the secondary team is that members belong to different professions. There may be professionals from a number of disciplines, for example teachers, physiotherapists, speech and language therapists and social workers. In addition, there will be non-professionals such as parents (who, it must be remembered, may be professionals in their other life). Professionals most closely identify with people in the same profession; so the teacher is most likely to identify with other teachers and the physiotherapist with other physiotherapists. A strong identification with these other members of the same profession, in terms of shared identity, shared values and a common language, can cause some problems with working in a multidisciplinary team. These can be summarised as follows:

- professionals are territorial;
- professionals have a private language;
- professionals see the world differently to each other; and
- professionals like autonomy and value their independence.

Professionals are territorial
Different professional groups are closely identified with different areas. So teachers may see their area of expertise as teaching and, more specifically, teaching reading and writing. Physiotherapists, on the other hand, may see their area of expertise as motor movement and, more specifically, positioning. There is little overlap between teachers' and physiotherapists' areas of expertise and, therefore, little risk of conflict. On the other hand, occupational therapists may see their area of expertise as fine motor skills. Their area of expertise overlaps with both teachers and physiotherapists. This may lead to conflict over which profession has expertise in this area. Professionals can become imperialists, trying to conquer territory and then defend their own boundaries. This may mean that different professional groups will try to claim similar territory, in terms of expertise, and to undervalue other professionals who are working in the same area.

Professionals have a private language
Not only do professionals have their own territory but they also have their own private language to talk about their territory. So when teachers talk about the development of children's writing skills in terms of progress on the National Curriculum and key stages reached, the vast majority of adults have little idea of what is actually meant. Similarly, when occupational therapists talk about children who resist external rotation when their legs are crossed, or the importance of neutral pelvic tilt, most adults have little idea of what is meant.

These different languages stem from the different theoretical perspectives of the professionals and make it difficult for different professionals to communicate with each other.

Professionals see the world differently to each other
This is only the start of the problem. Not only do different professionals have different languages to talk about the child's development, but they also actually see it differently. The language different professionals use actually influences the way they see the world. This may seem rather far-fetched but a famous example is of people's perception of snow (Whorf 1956). Eskimos have over 40 different words for snow. The argument is that they can, therefore, *see* over 40 different kinds of snow. On the other hand, in English there is the one word, 'snow' (and maybe a few more like 'sleet'), and therefore people who speak English do not see what Eskimos see.

Physiotherapists not only use different words, they actually sees things differently from the teacher. He can see things about the child's physical difficulties that the teacher can't see. Similarly, of course, the teacher can see things about the child's learning that the physiotherapist cannot see.

Working together effectively

Though there are difficulties working in the secondary multidisciplinary team, there are also tremendous advantages. Different professions' ability to see the world differently can mean a much deeper and broader perspective on the child's difficulties. So a multidisciplinary team working with a child with complex and multiple problems will see different ways in which the child can be helped.

Over time, an effective secondary team allows each professional new ways of seeing the child. To do this the team needs to meet regularly to allow a shared language to develop. The challenge for professionals is how to share their particular perspectives so that the rest of the team can see the problem in different ways.

Continuum of multidisciplinary teamwork
In recent years the secondary teams which are seen to work most effectively are those whose work is transdisciplinary (Fox 1998). A transdisciplinary team is one where the professionals work together – rather than in parallel. Transdisciplinary teamwork has implications not only for working together directly with the child, but also for setting collaborative goals, regular meetings and joint record-keeping on the child's progress (see Table 4.2).

One of the implications of working in a transdisciplinary way is that professionals work in areas that are traditionally associated with other disciplines. For example, the physiotherapist may spend time in the classroom working with the

Multidisciplinary teamwork	
Low-level, cross-disciplinary	• Professionals work with the child individually. • Targets are set individually by each professional. • Meetings with other professionals do not occur. • Records are kept and written individually.
Cross-disciplinary	• Professionals work with the child individually. • Targets are set individually by each professional. • Meetings are used to exchange information. • Reports are written individually.
Interdisciplinary	• Professionals work with the child individually. • Meetings share knowledge and set goals collaboratively. • Records are kept and written together.
Transdisciplinary	• Professionals work with the child together. • Meetings share knowledge, collaboratively set goals and develop new perspectives. • Single set of records is kept and written collaboratively.

Table 4.2   Multidisciplinary teamwork

child on his handwriting skills. The teacher could be working on the child's physical management programme, having a direct input into this side of the child's development. The TA could be teaching the child communication skills directly – not only supporting him in the classroom but also setting goals jointly with parents and other professionals.

This does not mean that professionals are not involved in their own areas of expertise; they are, but they share their expertise, language and unique perspectives with other members of the secondary team. Another aspect of transdisciplinary working is that professionals shift the levels at which they are working to suit the needs of the child. So a teacher might initially spend time working directly with the child before moving to a monitoring role while the TA takes on the direct teaching role. Or the direct teaching role might be taken on by the speech and language therapist if the child had particular difficulties articulating these sounds. The roles are not tied to the individual, rather they are shifting to make the best use of the time available.

The physical management programme

One of the key areas that the secondary team will need to work on together is the child's physical management programme. Chapter 2 outlined the different types of physical difficulties the child may have. For inclusion to be successful these difficulties need to be addressed as an integral part of the school day.

The secondary team should plan to meet the child's physical needs. Ideally, the first meeting should be before the child starts in a new class – though it might have to be in the first week of term. Subsequent meetings to review progress will need to be at least termly. The purpose of this meeting is to plan in detail how the physical management programme will be integrated into the school day. (Other areas that also need to be planned for – particularly communication and independence – can also be included in this meeting.) Once these three areas are established it then becomes possible for the core team to focus on progress on the National Curriculum.

How important is physical management?

One of the main issues for teachers is what prominence should the child's physical management programme take within an educational setting. How much time each day should go on the child's physical management? Exactly how important is the child's physical management? The answer is unfortunately similar to 'How long is a piece of string?' – it depends. What it depends *on* are the attitudes and aspirations of the child and the parents as well as the professionals surrounding the child. Children, though young, demonstrate through their involvement or lack of involvement with the physical management programme their attitude to it. The physical management programme can lead to boredom, frustration and behavioural problems in some children. This may be seen as a significant factor by some parents who will then modify the intensity of the programme because of their child's level of interest.

Other parents will be less susceptible to their child's influence. They will believe that the child is very young and needs to be forced or encouraged, even against his will, to participate. Finally, other significant adults – teachers and therapists – will influence both children and parents. Professionals can form a powerful relationship with both parents and children and can be a major influence on the importance that the physical management programme takes in the child's life.

Chapter 7 looks more closely at the issues of deciding on joint goals. It must be a collaborative decision about how the programme for physical management fits into the classroom planning for the child. However, many professionals involved in this area believe that after the age of 7, walking patterns are basically set and those children who are going to walk with or without assistance will have done so by this age. This is not to say that some children can improve their mobility skills after this age if taught systematically. As importantly, children will also lose skills after this age if they do not have a physical management programme. However, most agree that these first seven years are crucial.

Essential features of managing the child's physical difficulties

There are two essential features of managing the child's physical difficulties:

- the **development** of new physical skills; and
- the **maintenance** of existing physical skills.

Underpinning these is a third area. Some children will always require physical assistance. The focus of the programme is, then, on helping the child make decisions about this area. For example, a child may not be able to go to the toilet independently but he can decide *when* he wants to go. The focus is on ensuring that he can communicate about his physical needs.

The balance between the development and maintenance of physical skills will change during the child's development. In the early years great emphasis will be placed on the development of new skills. In particular, walking will often be at the forefront of both parents' and physiotherapists' minds. It is likely that they will want to put considerable time and effort into achieving this goal, or making steps towards it. By the time children are 7 or 8, it is clearer what physical skills they are likely to develop. The focus of the physical management programme becomes more one of maintaining existing skills.

The importance of maintaining physical skills

An able-bodied child is in a constant state of flux, positioning and repositioning, while sitting and walking around the classroom. For many children with physical difficulties such movements are impossible. So the first problem is that such children are static. Unless their bodies are moved passively, they will lose the strength and flexibility of their muscles.

The second problem is that, for some children, for example those with cerebral palsy, the body is being pulled into abnormal postures. If the child is left for too long in these positions these abnormal postures will turn into fixed difficulties (known as fixed-term deformities). These include:

- contractures, where there is permanent shortening of muscles and tendons;
- scoliosis, where the spine begins to become permanently curved and cannot then be straightened (apart from through surgery); and
- dislocation of the hips, where the hip bone comes out of the hip socket.

The third problem is sores. This can be a particular issue for children with spina bifida. With no feeling in the lower parts of their bodies, sores can develop quickly and become almost impossible to heal.

In addition, there can be a range of other problems associated with joints and connecting muscles. The physical management programme is not, therefore, simply a development programme but also a maintenance and preventative programme.

The core team's role in managing the child's physical difficulties

A number of different programmes for the development and maintenance of physical skills were outlined in Chapter 2. All these required direct work with the child. The physiotherapist is likely to take the lead in developing and implementing the physical management programme. However, the teacher and TA also have vital roles to play. These may involve

- agreeing targets for the physical management programme that will promote the child's learning;
- carrying out parts of the programme on a daily basis;
- using appropriate equipment; and
- being responsible for positioning the child in the classroom.

Positioning

Positioning is probably the key to helping children with physical difficulties both physically and educationally. The child needs to be in different positions for different purposes in education. So he needs to be positioned

- to prevent fixed difficulties (contractures, scoliosis etc.);
- to communicate;
- for independence – for example eating his lunch;
- for education – for example reading.

Positioning the child may involve the whole body or just one part, for example an arm. The benefit of good positioning is that it makes movements easier by making the body not to have to work against gravity. By making movement easier, it also means that the child has to use less conscious energy to maintain his position.

Good positioning means optimising symmetry and stability.

Symmetry is all about keeping both sides of the body even – the body being in midline. For many children with physical difficulties there is a tendency for the body to be pulled out of shape. This can be seen when the body is hunched towards the left or right. Not only does this cause long-term problems as outlined above, it also means that the child is not likely to be in the best position for learning and communication.

Stability is about the body being kept still. The more the body can be stabilised the less effort the child has to put into maintaining posture. The key aspect to maintaining stability is head control. For a child to learn he needs to be able to keep his head still. Without this he cannot focus on his work. He cannot read or focus on an activity in front of him. The secondary team need to consider both physically how the child is sitting and, secondly, what support/equipment may be best used. The head needs to be straight, in midline, possible bent slightly forward. Sitting upright helps the child maintain position. This means, once again, the body being in midline with the pelvis, hips, shoulder girdle and shoulders, stable and supported as required.

Special equipment may well support this optimal position of being symmetrical and stable. Such equipment is often the responsibility of an occupational therapist as well as the physiotherapist. Expensive equipment, such as an outdoor wheelchair, may be ideal for providing independent mobility, but it can be a hindrance to learning in the classroom. Different equipment may be required for different functions. The child may need

- a special, adapted front-leaning chair that allows different types of trunk support if the child cannot sit in an ordinary chair;
- a wheelchair if the child is not mobile around the classroom or school;
- a tilt table that can be adjusted to the child's sitting position; or
- a mobile stander for children who cannot stand for extended periods.

Issues for the core team

The teacher and TA need to clarify with the secondary team a number of issues. These include:

- How often should the child's position be changed if he can't do this by himself?
- How can we make him feel secure and stable in his position?
- How can we keep him symmetrical?
- Can we change his position if he is finding a task difficult?
- How do we lift the child?
- Where should we position equipment so that he can reach it?
- Should we be carrying out any exercises with the child? How do we do these?
- What members of the secondary team will work with us in the classroom to help us to deliver the physical management programme?

There may not be simple answers to some of these questions. The secondary team must, however, reach agreement on these issues so that the core team can manage the child's physical needs in the classroom.

The effective secondary team

For the child's physical management programme (and his communication and independence programme) to be integrated into the school day there needs to be effective transdisciplinary working. This means professionals have to work together with, for example, the physiotherapist working in the classroom. Targets for the child need to be set collaboratively in open meetings where everyone's perspective is valued. A single record needs to be kept on the child's progress – one that incorporates education, health, social services, voluntary agencies and the family's perspectives. All these ways of joined-up thinking can be difficult for professionals who are used to working independently. Professionals can feel vulnerable to criticism or not knowing what to do. It is important to acknowledge these difficulties if effective transdisicplinary working is to be established.

Summary

- The inclusion of children with physical difficulties depends on effective team-working.
- Teams help tackle difficult tasks and provide social and psychological support.
- Working with others opens up different ways of helping the child.
- The core team needs to plan and manage the child's development on a day-to-day basis.
- The secondary team needs to plan and manage the integration of the physical management programme (and other functional skills programmes) into the school day.
- The secondary team works most effectively if it is transdisciplinary.

CHAPTER 5

Working with the Child

Learning and relationships

Effective teaching focuses on both the child's learning and the teacher's relationship with the child. The focus on learning is about ensuring the development of the child's skills and abilities. The focus on the relationship is about meeting his psychological and social needs so that learning can occur.

For many children with physical difficulties these developments are closely interrelated with their communication skills. The development of a good relationship with the class teacher and TA depends upon developing effective communication. However, the development of good communication depends upon building a good relationship between the adult and child. In both these areas the child with a physical difficulty presents some particular challenges for the teacher. These can be divided into five areas:

- building a relationship with a child with a physical difficulty;
- building interactional skills with a child with severe physical difficulties;
- understanding the child's cognitive-linguistic development when he has severe physical difficulties;
- developing augmentative and alternative communication skills when the child has limited or no speech; and
- using Personal Passports for the child to develop communication and relationships both within and outside the classroom.

The focus in this chapter is largely on children with severe communication difficulties which are associated with severe physical difficulties.

Building the relationship

The teacher needs to build a psycho-social relationship with the child with a physical difficulty in the same way as she does with all children in her class. There are three crucial aspects of good relationships (Egan 1990). These are respect, genuineness and empathy.

Respect

Teachers show respect for the child when they show that he is valued. For a child with a physical disability this can be shown through:

- celebrating and acknowledging his differences;
- caring about his wellbeing; and
- giving the pupil time and attention.

Teachers demonstrate this respect through their interactions with the child. Children with physical difficulties often take more time than the other children in the class. A teacher who takes the time to listen without interrupting demonstrates, in a simple and practical way, that she respects him.

Genuineness

By being herself the teacher shows she is genuine. This means not putting unnecessary barriers between herself and the child. Teachers show that they are genuine when they are:

- open – willing to acknowledge when they don't have the answer;
- consistent in values and behaviour – not saying one thing and doing another; and
- spontaneous – laughing when something is funny!

Teachers demonstrate their genuineness when they don't put on masks when placed in difficult situations. Having a child with a physical disability in a mainstream class can be very difficult. Acknowledging those difficulties and working on them is much more genuine than pretending that they don't exist.

Empathy

Empathy is about understanding another person's world. Teachers are empathetic when they show that they understand how the child feels. Sometimes a simple statement demonstrates that empathy: 'You seem upset because the others won't play with you.' 'It must make you angry when you keep dropping your pen.'

The statement 'You feel . . . because . . .' demonstrates that the teacher has some understanding of the feelings of the child with a physical difficulty. However, empathy is not simply a communication technique for teachers to use. It is really understanding what it is like for the child, even though the teacher does not have a physical difficulty.

Teachers show a high concern for the child by using these three skills in the classroom. Underpinning them all is the need for the child to have 'unconditional positive regard' (Rogers 1983). This is to be thought well of or, put more strongly, to feel loved for just being himself. For the child with a physical difficulty this may be particularly important. He needs to know that being different, being in a wheel-chair or having no speech does not make a difference to whether the teacher feels positive about him.

There are, however, some particular problems with building this respectful, genuine and empathetic relationship with the child with a physical difficulty.

The role of the disabled child

Transactional Analysis (TA) (Champeau 1992) is a particular useful way of making sense of the relationships between people. TA distinguishes three roles people can take in their interactions with each other. These are: parent; adult; child. The roles do not refer to the age of the person; teachers plays all the roles at some time or other during the school day as do parents and children. Aspects of all the roles can be helpful at times and they can also be problematic.

The parent role

Everyone takes on the parent role at some time – including the child. People take on the parent role when they feel, think or act as they saw their parents act when they were little. The parent can act as controlling or critical, nurturing or loving. So the little boy on the playground who comforts his crying friend by telling him to be brave is playing the parent role.

The adult role

When people decide how to behave by thinking analytically, gathering and using information they are in the adult role. Facts and reasons are used to make deci-sions. The same boy who suggests to the teacher that because it is raining they will need to have a wet break is playing the adult role.

The child role

Even teachers have a child inside them! When a person reacts spontaneously and emotionally they are being as they were as a child. The child is dependent and looks for how to behave and think from the parents or adults. The boy who is now sulking in the corner having been told off is playing the child role.

Sometimes people deliberately play a role. The newly qualified teacher may feel, and be told, that they must now look like a teacher and take on a parental role in terms of controlling the children in the class. Over time, the teacher may no longer be conscious that she is playing a role, but finds instead that it takes over her life, so that she finds herself playing the teacher at a friend's Christmas party.

The role a person takes is interdependent on the role other people take. A teacher can get locked into communicating with a colleague in a particular way because the other person always responds in the same way. This can be a particular issue for the child with a physical difficulty and his teacher.

When the child starts school he is likely to play the child role. This will be the expectation of the teacher who, in turn, plays the parent role. However, the physical dependence of the child may lock them into these roles for longer than is helpful; both sides in the transaction reinforce the child's dependency. If the child is to move to a less dependent position he needs to move away from the adult–child relationship. This can be considerably difficult, not only because of his physical dependency but also because of the nature of the usual relationship within schools.

Over time, three patterns of transactions can develop between the teacher and the child.

Pattern 1: pupil in adult role/teacher in parent role. The pupil makes an effort to be independent and to move to an adult position. The teacher, however, is unable to reciprocate and continues to act in the parent role. An example of this is the pupil who wishes to use his sticks within the playground. His teacher, however, insists that he uses his wheelchair, as he will be safer. Another example is the pupil who wants to work independently but the TA believes that she should sit beside him and help.

Pattern 2: teacher in adult role/pupil in child role. The teacher makes an effort to help the child be independent by moving to an adult position. The pupil, however, is unable to reciprocate and stays stuck in the child position. For example, the teacher encourages the pupil only to use the toilet at break times. The pupil, however, wants to use the toilet during lessons.

Pattern 3: pupil in child role/teacher in parent role. Both the pupil and the teacher have difficulty changing from the original child–parent relationship. For example, the pupil does not want to do PE. The teacher agrees with this and the pupil sits on the side of the hall while the class has PE. Another example is when the pupil is due to move to secondary school. Both pupil and teacher become excessively protective about this change of school, feeling that the child will not be able to cope.

The first two of the above patterns may result in conflict between the teacher and the child. The last pattern results in chronic over-dependence. The teacher needs to be aware how the role she takes may increase the child's dependency. She needs to shift into taking an adult role as regards the child with a physical difficulty. This means being clear about the needs the child has and being empathetic to his position. However, it does not mean becoming overwhelmed emotionally and simply feeling sorry for the child or angry at the system for not helping the child to develop. By taking on the adult role the teacher shows respect, genuineness and empathy and helps the child to develop as an adult.

The emphasis so far in this chapter has been on developing a positive relationship with a child with a physical difficulty when they have good communication skills. Essentially the child needs to be treated in the same way as all other children by using respect, genuineness and empathy. Care needs to be maintained to ensure that inappropriate roles are not taken on because of the child's physical difficulty. Most teachers feel relatively confident about working with children with good communication skills. However, some children with severe physical difficulties have very limited communication when they start school. Building a relationship with these children is the focus of the next section.

Building interactional skills

Key features of communication

A relationship between the child and the teacher cannot develop without some type of communication. Communication has a number of important features:

- It largely occurs verbally through language. However, there is also a significant non-verbal component, for example gesture and movement.
- Communication in the classroom is not just about knowledge and facts; communication can be about the whole range of experiences. It can be about feelings and behaviours as well as conceptual or procedural knowledge.
- Communication is a two-way process. Either the teacher or the child can initiate an interaction and then the other will (or can) respond. The child is not just a passive recipient of the teacher's communication. The child can also start an interaction and engage the teacher in a sequence of responses. This is known as 'two-way alternating dialogue' (Newson 1979).

A small example illustrates these aspects of communication. The teacher asks a question, the child looks up at the teacher and puts up his hand, the teacher nods at him, signalling that he can talk, the child gives an answer and the teacher says 'well done' and looks away, the child smiles at the teacher and the teacher asks if there is anything that he would like to add, the child responds. In this brief sequence, verbal and non-verbal communication is taking place. Both the teacher and the child initiate parts of the sequence and the communication is about feelings, behaviour and knowledge. Many variations of this interaction go on hundreds of times every day in the classroom. Learning takes place in this dynamic social environment.

Issues of communicating with a child with a physical difficulty

Interactions between teachers and a child with a physical difficulty may be different from the preceding example (Mahoney 1988). One of the reasons that interactions are different is that the child's physical difficulty may make it difficult or impossible for him to act and react in the same way as the able-bodied child. So he may not be able to put his hand up or make eye contact. Not only may there be differences in these non-verbal skills, but the child may also have difficulties with his speech. So the child's reply to a question may be to grimace and make a very loud vocal noise which the teacher cannot understand.

The other reason that the interaction may be different is that the teacher may act or react differently to the child with a physical difficulty. So she may not look at him to cue an answer or she may not find the time to wait for an answer. The whole sequential nature of communication may be lost. In addition, there may be organisational issues, such as the teacher not being able to see the child's communication board, or the child not being able to reposition himself to see the teacher.

These differences may mean that interaction, instead of being pleasurable, can be difficult and stressful (McCollum 1984). If it is not pleasurable, over time changes in interaction may occur. The child may initiate fewer interactions and withdraw into inactivity. The teacher can also feel helpless and unable to communicate with the child. She may compensate for this feeling of helplessness by withdrawing. So, over time, the teacher may initiate fewer and fewer interactions with the child, believing it is more appropriate to leave it to the teaching assistant.

The particular danger for the TA is then to become too intrusive and verbally directive (Clark and Seifer 1983). If the child's physical difficulties get in the way of him initiating, responding and maintaining interaction, the TA carries more of the interaction burden. The TA can soon be not only initiating the interaction but also responding. This is not to blame the TA, who is trying to be sensitive and responsive in order to help the child participate in the classroom. Initially, it may be very helpful for the TA to show high levels of initiation and to be directing and maintaining the interaction. However, over time, the burden must not simply remain with the adult; it needs to be gradually taken up by the child, otherwise he simply learns to be helpless and remains in the child role.

The fundamentals of communication

To motivate young children with severe physical difficulties to communicate, the TA (or teacher) can use a series of techniques based on Intensive Interaction (Nind and Hewett 1994). These mirror the sort of reciprocal interaction that mothers have with their babies. They provide a very useful basis for the development of interaction with a child, which fundamentally shows respect for the child, and encourages the TA to initiate and maintain the interaction.

The following techniques provide a basis for beginning to develop communication skills:

- **permission**: sit or crouch near the child. Make certain your head is at or below his eye level.
- **mutual enjoyment**: make eye contact and smile. Demonstrate through your face that this interaction with you is going to be fun.
- **watching and waiting**: observe the child. Wait for him to initiate interaction. Depending on his communication skills this may be through vocalisation, finger-pointing to a communication board or eye-pointing.
- **translation**: put into words what you understand by his communication – 'Oh . . . Yes it's raining outside.'
- **watching and waiting**: observe the child. Wait for his affirmation or disconfirmation of your translation. Wait for him to elaborate on his initial interaction.
- **clarify and/or elaborate**: develop the child's idea by either clarifying aspects of it or elaborating it by adding to it – 'I think the playground will be wet with big puddles of water.'
- **ask questions**: questions can be either open or closed. Closed questions – to obtain more information – are much easier for a child with communication difficulties – 'Do you want to stay inside if it is raining?' Be careful about using open questions unless the child has good methods of communication.

The purpose of this strategy is to help the child engage in an interaction. It aims to let the child lead the interaction so that he can have some sense of power and a belief that the teacher and TA are listening. In addition, the child with severe physical difficulties and no speech needs to learn one simple skill in order to be able to communicate effectively. He needs to learn to 'point' consistently. This 'pointing' can be done with a finger, a hand or simply by looking. Eye-pointing is when the child looks in particular directions to communicate. For example, the child can eye-point by looking up for 'Yes', and looking down for 'No'. This is sufficient to communicate effectively when used in conjunction with an Augmentative or Alternative Communication system (AAC), which is discussed in detail later in the chapter.

Implications for teachers for building interactional skills

Interaction is used for different purposes in the classroom. It is used for learning and building a relationship. For children with physical difficulties the interaction process is atypical. For some children with severe physical difficulties even simple interactions can be extremely difficult. A process of interaction needs to be developed by the teacher and TA that empowers the child. Crucial for developing this interactional style is the need of the teacher to

- join the child with his interests;
- be playful;
- build on any communication; and
- recognise that nothing specific has to be learnt during the interaction.

Developing the child's ability to interact involves two people, the child and the adult. The problem is that the child will initiate and interact less and less over time unless the teacher gives him the motivation to communicate.

Understanding the child's cognitive-linguistic development

Language has two functions: to communicate externally with other people and also internally for thinking. The development of cognitive (or thinking) ability and language are intertwined. This is known as cognitive-linguistic development. One of the great debates in developmental psychology is how much a child can think without language. Language is about the use of symbols. These symbols can be verbal but they can also be non-verbal, writing or signs.

Speech and language

An issue for many children with physical difficulties is with producing speech. This is particularly true for children with cerebral palsy who often have difficulties with articulation, known as *dysarthria*. Spasticity of the speech muscles leads to slow, laboured speech and difficulty controlling the tongue which may be thrust frequently out of the mouth (Hall and Hill 1996). The child's speech may be limited to a few different sounds or it may be more developed but still very difficult to understand. Communication is affected by these difficulties with speech. However, there is no reason to assume that the child's language is affected. It is language that is connected with thought, not speech. There is, therefore, no reason to think that a child's speech difficulties will affect his cognitive-linguistic ability.

Children with physical disabilities may also appear to have a receptive language problem because of these difficulties with speech. The child who is very slow in

Speech	Tick one
Speech at an age-appropriate level	
Some difficulties with understanding language	
Considerable difficulties in understanding language	
Very limited speech	
Some vocalisation	

Table 5.1 Speech skills: checklist for teachers

responding, either vocally or through a gesture, may appear not to understand what the teacher is saying. The teacher needs to give considerable extra time when waiting for a response.

However, a child with a physical difficulty, like able-bodied children, may have a receptive language problem. This is more likely if the physical difficulty is neurologically based (for example cerebral palsy). If a child has significant difficulties understanding language then specialist assessment in this area is required. This will include checking hearing as children with physical difficulties and a hearing problem are often mis-assessed as having a receptive language problem. The other concern for teachers is that the child who appears not to understand language may have general cognitive-linguistic difficulties.

Table 5.1 provides a checklist for speech skills.

Cognitive ability

A common concern for teachers is whether the child with a physical difficulty has the ability to learn at the same rate as his peers. In other words, does the child with a physical difficulty also have a learning difficulty in terms of progression on the National Curriculum? There are a number of reasons why teachers may make this assumption:

- **difficulties with communication** – the child may take a long time to respond to the teacher's question;
- **difficulties with speech** – the teacher may have difficulties understanding the child's speech;
- **difficulties with writing** – the child may find it difficult to draw or write and, therefore, to communicate in other ways;
- **difficulties with independence** – the dependency of the child in terms, for

example, of eating and toileting may make the teacher feel he is younger than he is; and

- **difficulties with physical skills** – age-inappropriate physical skills, for example drooling, may make the child appear younger than he is.

Cognitive development

The lack of activity and play by the child may also reinforce teachers' concerns about cognitive development. One of the fundamental beliefs about early years education, especially nursery education, is that children develop their cognitive thinking skills through play. Early years educators believe that it is through play that children's cognitive structures or processes develop in the brain (Piaget 1966). Activities which involve the handling of objects – such as matching shapes, sorting colours and ordering objects by size – are all examples of learning activities that stem from such beliefs.

What then are the implications for a child whose physical skills mean that he cannot play? There are many children with physical difficulties who cannot reach, hold or release objects. How does this affect their cognitive development? The answer appears to be that it does not. There have been a small number of studies of children who because of their physical difficulties are unable to manipulate objects (Kopp and Shaperman 1973; Cioni *et al.* 1993). These studies show that children with physical difficulties go through the same stages of cognitive development and develop the same cognitive skills as the able-bodied, even though they cannot play in the same way.

These findings go directly against the fundamental assumption that the child has to be able to play with objects to develop his cognitive structures. However, what children who cannot play require is the opportunity to observe other children playing with and manipulating objects. The teaching implication of this is that even if the child with a physical difficulty is unable to do an activity he should not be excluded from it. Instead he will learn through observation if he is able to see the activity being performed.

Children with physical disabilities may have cognitive difficulties that are difficulties with learning. However, it is important to be aware of how children with physical difficulties may be wrongly considered to have cognitive difficulties because of other factors.

Assessing cognitive ability

Standardised tests

Traditionally, children's cognitive abilities have been assessed using standardised psychometric tests. These psychometric tests are designed to measure the child's abilities in a variety of areas and to produce a General IQ (Intelligence Quotient) score. The IQ of a child compares what he achieved on this test with other children of the same age. These standardised tests often divide the General IQ into two components, a Verbal IQ and a Performance IQ. Psychometric tests have received considerable criticism over the last few decades. This criticism focuses on a number of areas. The validity of IQ tests in terms of them actually defining what intelligence is has been questioned. The reliability of the IQ in terms of whether the same score would be obtained regardless of who administered the test, and on what day, is also a criticism. More fundamentally, IQ tests are seen to discriminate against particular groups of children and to be confused with measuring the child's innate and unalterable ability. Despite these criticisms, standardised IQ tests continue to be used widely in education, with some LEAs continuing to use ability test scores for the allocation of secondary schools.

Difficulties with standardised tests
There are some obvious additional difficulties with using psychometric tests with children with physical difficulties. Many items are timed, which can be a particular difficulty for children with speech and motor difficulties. In addition, some items require considerable fine motor skills – a particular issue for children with physical difficulties. Despite these difficulties standardised assessments can be extremely helpful to the class teacher. In a paradoxical way the more severe the child's physical difficulties and the more limited their communication the more likely it is that a psychometric assessment can be helpful to the teacher. For a child with severe physical difficulties and no speech, being able to demonstrate that his understanding of language is appropriate for his age can be vital to successful inclusion in the classroom.

Understanding the child
One way of assessing a child's understanding is to use tests such as the BPVT (British Picture Vocabulary Test). This consists of a series of cards, each containing four pictures. One of the pictures is named and the child is asked to indicate which picture is being referred to. The test becomes increasingly difficult, with more complex and unfamiliar words being used. The level of the child's understanding is then compared with children of the same age.

There are other tests which assess the child's non-linguistic ability. One of these – the Raven's Coloured Progressive Matrices – identifies children's ability to recognise shapes and patterns – their visual-spatial ability.

The benefit of these types of assessment is that the child has only to have minimal communication skills to be able to complete them. A child has only to be able to eye-point or indicate 'Yes' or 'No'. These tests can also be adapted by enlarging the page or cutting out the pictures in order to move them further apart. This allows even the child with poor eye-pointing to indicate the correct answer.

Standardised tests can also be used to assess functional skills such as reading. For the child without speech, reading fluency cannot be assessed. However, reading comprehension *can* be assessed using reading passages from standardised tests such as the MacMillan (Vincent and de la Mare 1985). The child's comprehension is tested by giving him a number of possible answers. He has to indicate which answer is correct.

Assessment through teaching

One of the most effective ways of assessing cognitive-linguistic ability is through teaching. Reading is often the focus for this teaching. For example, the child can be taught an initial sight vocabulary. The ease with which he learns this gives some indication of his ability.

However, some children with physical difficulties, particularly those with cerebral palsy, may have particular visual processing difficulties (see Chapter 2). This may mean that it is particularly difficult for them to learn to read. This does not mean that they have general learning difficulties but very particular ones associated with trying to make sense of visual representations. This means that letters or words can often appear backwards. The letters may not seem to hold together as they do for most children. It is important that these specific visual-perceptual difficulties a child may have are not confused with general learning difficulties. Unfortunately, for some children with physical difficulties there are relatively few opportunities for them to demonstrate their learning. Teachers need to be particularly vigilant with these children so that they do not misread a lack of progression in a particular curriculum area as a general learning difficulty.

Factors affecting learning

The child's ability may well affect his learning. However, there are a range of other factors that are equally, if not more, important when considering the learning of children with physical difficulties. These factors include:

- the amount of time in the school day that goes into independence needs and physical management;
- the amount of time missing from school;
- their tiredness given these other pressures;
- their dependence on others to move around;
- their dependence on others to initiate and maintain interaction; and
- the expectations of teachers about what can be achieved.

Some children with physical difficulties do also have learning difficulties. However, many do not. It is important not to confuse such difficulties with problems with communication or specific visual-perceptual difficulties. It is only through careful

Does the child have difficulties with communication?

Sub-area	Yes	No	Don't know	Comments
Interactional skills				
Speech				
Comprehension				

Does the child have learning difficulties?

Sub-area	Yes	No	Don't know	Comments
In all subjects				
In specific areas				
Reading				
Mathematics				
Writing				

Table 5.2 Summary of cognitive-linguistic difficulties

structured teaching, over time, that the potential of many of these children can really be understood.

Developing augmentative and alternative communication skills

For children with severe physical difficulties, developing their communication skills is fundamental to their education. Many children with physical difficulties use some kind of aid to help them to communicate. These are known as Augmentative or Alternative Communications aids (AAC). Most LEAs have a specialist advisory teacher who works in conjunction with the local speech and language therapists to advise on AAC systems. However, it is the class teacher and TA, who use them on a daily basis, who are often in the best position to ensure that they are used effectively.

Augmentative and alternative aids are often the same; however, it is helpful to remember that they may have different purposes. Augmentative aids are used to support speech, alternative aids are used to replace it.

The aim of AAC is to ensure that the child is able to function effectively. It should enable him to initiate communication, to make choices and to be able to

Types of communication	Tick
Eye-pointing	
Gesture	
Vocalisation (non-speech)	
Sign language	
Augmentative – Low-tech	
Augmentative – High-tech	
Speech	

Table 5.3   Checklist for teachers: types of communication

respond to teachers and peers. In other words, it has social and emotional, as well as educational, functions. Though aspects of it may be specific to the classroom it must be a total communication system that the child can use in the playground, after school, at home and on holiday.

The teacher needs to think about AAC in two areas:

- How can this child's use of the AAC system be improved?
- How can this child's skills using the AAC be used to access the curriculum?

The first is about developing the child's use of the AAC system. The second is about ensuring the child uses the system to access the curriculum.

Table 5.3 provides a communication checklist.

Augmentative and alternative systems

Sign language, as used by deaf children, is the most common AAC system but it is usually not suitable for children with physical difficulties as it requires good hand skills. The most common type of AAC system for children with physical disabilities is communication aids. These are all, essentially, systems that display information which the child, and the adults and peers that they come in contact with, can access. AACs are divided into what is known as high- and low-tech aids. **Low-tech aids** include such things as communication boards, picture folders and notebooks. They are relatively cheap to make and can be made by the school and at home. **High-tech aids** are usually made commercially, electronic or computer-based, and are relatively expensive. Some high-tech aids are specifically dedicated to communication, for example the AlphaTalker and the Digivox. On the other hand, some high-tech aids are part of a multipurpose system. These serve more functions than communication and may, for example, also have a computer interface for educational use. Some of these systems can be used as computers themselves, allowing the child to use word-processing skills. Examples of multipurpose systems include Real Voice, the Touch Talker/Light Talker and the Liberator.

There are three basic questions about communication aids that teachers need to know about. These are:

- How is the information represented?
- How is the aid accessed?
- What is the means of output?

How is the information represented?

The way the information is represented on either a high-tech or low-tech aid depends on the age of the child as well as his other skills, for example cognitive, visual and physical. So the representation can be in the form of photographs, pictures, line drawings, symbols or words (see Table 5.4). The young child might start with photographs and pictures with the aim of progressing to using symbols and words. Moving to symbols and words allows the child to communicate more complex information. It also, in itself, facilitates the development and monitoring of the child's cognitive-linguistic skills.

The communication aid's complexity is created by having access to different levels of information. So for a young child, the first page might have pictures of different activities – the dressing-up corner, painting and musical instruments. If the child indicated the musical instrument, this page would be turned to. On this page there could be photographs of the different musical instruments that were available in the classroom. Once again, the child could indicate which one he wanted to play. Another page could then indicate different songs for the child to select from, and so on. This would be an example of a low-tech aid where there are literally separate sheets of paper which have to be turned manually by the teacher or TA.

It can be seen that such a system soon becomes unmanageable for complex curriculum areas. This is where a high-tech communication board is useful. Here the information is stored electronically and the child can move from page to page electronically, indicating what he wants to communicate. With the development of computers, new and exciting opportunities keep opening up. So, for example, word prediction can be used for the child who can read. This means that as the child begins to spell out a word, various possibilities are flashed up on the screen. These types of developments are making it quicker for children with physical difficulties to communicate.

Type of representation	Able to use	Unable to use	Do not know	Comments
Photographs				
Pictures				
Line drawings				
Symbols				
Words				

Table 5.4   Types of representation

How is the aid accessed?

There are two ways the child can access the communication aid: direct selection and scanning.

Direct selection: This is when the child directly accesses the picture or word that he wants to communicate. This direct access is usually done through touching or eye-pointing. It can also be done with the help of an aid – for example a head-pointer. Though this is the fastest method, it is also the most tiring. Direct selection should be the method of access whenever possible. The method of accessing affects the way the information is laid out. For a child who can only eye-point it may mean that only four items can be on any one page. These need to be placed in the corner of the page so that the teacher can easily see which one the child is eye-pointing to.

Scanning: This is an indirect method of access. It can be used in either low- or high-tech systems. Scanning in a low-tech system is when the adult moves her finger along the page. As she moves her finger over the various options she says aloud what each one is. The child indicates, for example with a nod of the head, when the desired activity is reached. For high-tech aids scanning works, in principle, in exactly the same way, though this time it is done electronically. The high-tech system automatically scans the sheet. The child has to indicate, usually by pressing a switch, when the desired item has been reached. Scanning is time-consuming and difficult for both the child and the listener. New communication aids have introduced time-saving features, for example predictive scanning, which stops the aid scanning empty locations.

	Yes	No	Don't know	Comments
Is direct selection used?				
Is indirect selection used?				
Is a switch used?				

Table 5.5   Accessing the aid

Scanning should only be used when the child does not have sufficient control over any part of his body to use direct selection. It is much more laborious and time-consuming for both the child and the recipient.

Switches
For many high-tech aids the method of access is through a switch. A switch enables electrical connection between two contacts. The switch can be connected to almost any electronic device. They can be used with AAC aids, but also with toys, common electrical equipment, such as TV sets, and environmental controls.

The head, a hand or any part of the body that the child can reliably move can operate a switch. They can even be operated by blowing. Some switches are activated simply by touching, whereas others need to be held down to remain operational. Many switches can be adjusted for the amount of movement or pressure required to activate them.

Table 5.5 provides a format for analysing access to aids.

What is the means of output?

There are two primary means of output – visual and auditory. Visual output can be either a high- or low-tech aid. Visual output means the teacher needs to be able to see the child's communication board. The record will be transient – the point of a finger at a picture or a word. With the high-tech aid the visual output can be permanent. So the computer can display a written message on its monitor which can then be printed off.

Auditory output is used with high-tech aids. It can take two forms – digitised speech and synthesised speech.

Synthesised speech is computer-generated speech. It uses the phonic rules of language to turn written phonemes into computer-generated sounds. It is often criticised as sounding like a 'Dalek'. Though it is being improved all the time, it often sounds monotone, as it cannot convey emotion.

	Yes	No	Don't know	Comments
Is visual output used?				
Is synthetic speech used?				
Is digitised speech used?				

Table 5.6   Means of output

Digitised speech is digitally recorded human speech. The quality of digital speech can vary depending on the quality of the recording and the capability of the communication aid. Digitised speech can incorporate accents and is much more emotional than synthetic speech. The problem is that it takes up much more storage space. Communication aids can often only store a few minutes of digitised speech, and even computers need considerable memory to be able to use it.

Table 5.6 helps to assess means of output.

Supporting written communication

AAC is an example of enabling, or assistive, technology. For pupils with physical difficulties enabling technology is increasingly providing more sophisticated strategies for children with more severe physical difficulties to access the curriculum.

Many children with even mild physical difficulties find handwriting difficult. These difficulties with recording work may make them seem less able than they really are. One simple way of tackling this issue is through provision of a word-processor. At its most simple, the word-processor can be used simply as an alternative to writing. For the child with a physical difficulty there are a range of adaptations that can be made for accessing a computer (see Table 5.7).

Voice-activated software
Voice-activated software can be very useful for children with significant fine motor difficulties but good speech. There are two main types of voice-activated software: speaker-independent systems and speaker-dependent systems.

Speaker-independent systems work without the child having to 'train up' the system. They can be used for a voice-activated switch or for environmental controls such as turning on and off lights, a radio or a TV set.

The second type, the speaker-dependent system, has to be trained to recognise the child's voice. An example of these is a Voice Navigation System which can be used to operate a computer, for example opening a document. In other words these systems allow the child to operate the computer by voice alone. A more sophisti-

Problem	Yes	No	Solution	Comment
Keyboard too small			Use expanded keyboard Use overlay on keyboard	
Keyboard too big			Use palm top	
Difficulty pressing the right key			Use keyguard	
Can't use keyboard			Replace with mouse and on-screen keyboard	
Difficulties with controlling mouse			Adjust control panel to slow pointer speed	
Difficulties with double-click, and click and drag on mouse			Replace mouse with programmable trackerball	
Difficulties using mouse at all			Use overlay keyboards to perform simple programs	
Difficulties with consistently using any fine motor movement			Use voice-activated software	

Table 5.7   Adaptations for accessing a computer (adapted from Rahamin 1999)

cated type of software is Speech Dictation systems. Once trained, the child simply can speak and the computer transforms the sounds into words. To train a Speech Dictation system the child has to read passages until the computer recognises his particular voice patterns. Voice-activated software offers much to a child with a physical difficulty who has good speech. However, for many children with physical disabilities their difficulties with speech mean that they cannot train a Speech Dictation system. They find it easier to type than they do to speak.

AAC in the classroom

The preceding section has outlined the basics of AAC. What are the implications of this for the teacher?

- the child is likely to have a high- and a low-tech aid;
- the child will need to be taught how to use the aids;

- the child will have to use the aids to access the National Curriculum;
- the teacher needs support from other professionals to develop the use of the AAC;
- the child's AAC needs are not static and need to be regularly reviewed. The teacher's input into this review is vital.

AAC is a highly specialised area of work and the class teacher will need to work with specialists in the area. However, the danger is that the AAC technology may get in the way of communication. As well as the sophisticated AAC technology there needs to be user-friendly means to ensure that the child communicates. One helpful mechanism to ensure this communication is the use of Personal Passports.

Using Personal Passports

The Personal Passport is a document that provides key practical information about the child (CALL 1997). Fundamentally, it provides information about what is needed to help him to communicate. Personal Passports are particularly useful when the child is starting in a new situation, where staff do not know him; so, for example, when starting school or moving from an infant to a junior school. Often the really important basic information that will help the child is not communicated in a way that is most helpful. The formal advice, as contained in the Statement or the Annual Review (see Chapter 7), does not contain this type of personal information.

Personal Passports have a number of key features:

- information is presented in the first person;
- information is presented in an empowering way, showing the child's uniqueness and individuality; and
- information is selective – what others really need to know (not everything).

In the example in Figure 5.1, the child is communicating about his prerequisites for being able to communicate. He is also communicating that he is an individual who wants to communicate. He is showing his individuality and his sense of humour. All these are important. This type of communicating is very different from an announcement by the SENCO in the staff meeting or a letter from the parents. This provides some details on exactly what the child needs to be able to communicate.

Personal Passports can contain pictures and photos as well as words. So a Passport might contain photos of the child's family or a diagram showing the best position for sitting at a desk.

The Personal Passport can give more information than just about communica-

Before I talk to you, I need to get a few things organised. Please help!

- I need the tray to be fixed to my wheelchair

- I need my communication chart on the tray

- I need you to stop walking and talking (or anything else) and to pay attention for a few minutes

> I know that last bit is hard. But just imagine what **you** would feel like if nobody ever had time to listen to you ...

Figure 5.1   Personal Passport – communication (adapted from CALL 1997)

tion. In the second example, in Figure 5.2, the child is communicating about his physical difficulties and the most effective way of managing them. This lets the child's peers, as well as any adults that he comes into contact with, understand how to manage his physical needs.

Two things are achieved by creating the Personal Passport. In the first instance, it provides a focus for the teacher and TA to discuss with the parents the most important aspects of managing the child – his communication, physical needs, independence, etc. Doing so is not only about sharing information, it also may lead to changes in attitudes and an increase in confidence by the staff as they feel they know the child better.

Once the Passport is complete the teacher and TA will have a much clearer idea about what is required in different situations. By writing down this information it then allows others to become involved more appropriately. So the child's peers in the class can understand that it is OK to hold his hand or that they need to give

---

If I keep telling you that I am uncomfy ask me if I'd like to come out of my chair for a stretch. I can relax quickly when I lie on the floor.

If my arm begins to wave about, don't worry. It is just relaxing and doesn't bother me at all. WATCH OUT that I don't hit you or knock your specs off by mistake!!

If it drives you crazy or disturbs a lesson, ask me if you may hold my arm gently.

(CALL 1997)

Figure 5.2   Personal Passport – physical needs

him more time to speak. Other members of staff and parents also then find it easier to begin to communicate and to take a more active role in the child's education.

The Personal Passport helps to ensure that:

- there is consistency in how different people understand and approach the child;
- new staff and pupils have a starting point for communication;
- parents' views are valued;
- teachers discuss with parents and others the best way of communicating with the child;
- the child's communication abilities are maximised; and
- information is made accessible and effective.

The third example of a Personal Passport shows how information on a variety of areas can be combined together (see Figure 5.3).

The examples of Personal Passports have all been single sheets. Most Personal Passports consist of a number of sheets presented as a booklet. If the Personal Passport is to be of value then care and attention needs to go into the booklet – it is not some quickly scribbled notes by the teacher. Try to ensure the booklet is quite sturdy – it should be handled on a daily basis. It also should be attractive, with limited information contained on each page. It is helpful if it contains some blank sheets – an invitation for others to add information.

Each Passport is individualised but some possible pages are:

- communication – how you can communicate with me;
- movement – how you can help me move around the school;
- independence – how you can help me be independent;
- timetable – how my timetable is different to the rest of the class;
- likes and dislikes – how to know what I like to do;
- specific information – procedures for medication, or if I am having a fit;
- relationships – who I like to sit near.

> Hi, my name is Robert
> I can understand everything that you are saying,
> But as I have cerebral palsy I cannot speak. I
> can let you know my feelings and wishes, and
> make decisions using my eyes (see 'Talk to me').
> In my bag there is a book. It will let you know things and
> so help you to get to know me.

Talk to me

If you ask me questions, I can answer using my eyes, 'Eye pointing'. An easy 'Look at Me' if I agree with what you are saying is 'Robert, look at me if you've seen East Enders'. For more details on ways I can communicate, please turn to page 3 in my book.

Manners

It is easy to see I have excellent manners. Please ask me if you want to touch me, move me or look at my belongings. If you want to look at my book, ask me first.

Include me too

I like to be included in everything that is going on, as I'm so friendly and have a good sense of fun. I have a lot of friends, and I'm very loyal to them.

Don't forget!

Though I can't talk, I'm not stupid. I'm pretty much on the ball. You better believe it!

Figure 5.3 Personal Passport – introduction page (adapted from CALL 1997)

It may be important that a single, laminated sheet is on display – for example on the child's desk. This can reference the rest of the Passport, a booklet which is kept inside the desk, in a school bag or with the teacher. The intention of the Person Passport is not to put the child on display but simply to give them a method of communication, which allows others to interact with them.

Summary

For the teacher to be effective she needs to build a good relationship with the child. This relationship depends on respect, genuineness and empathy. In addition, the teacher needs to

- be aware of the different roles she and the child can take which may reinforce dependence;

- develop and use different interactional skills;
- recognise the child's cognitive-linguistic development;
- develop augmentative and alternative communication skills;
- use additional technology in the classroom; and
- develop Personal Passports with the child to ensure peers and other adults develop their skills in communicating with the child.

CHAPTER 6

Making Friends

The importance of friends

Education, for all children, is more than about making progress on the National Curriculum; it is also about making friends and developing socially and emotionally. This chapter explores the issue of making friends from the perspective of a child with a physical difficulty. Friends are important for all children. They are particularly important to children with physical difficulties because they may have had fewer opportunities to interact with their peers than have the able-bodied. Their preschool life may have consisted largely of interacting with their family and the professionals who have given them treatment. They need friends to share and develop interests, to listen to ideas and feelings, and to develop passions – even if that is only for Manchester United.

Chapter 3 outlines how parents' greatest concerns about inclusion are to do with relationships with peers. Parents recognise that having friends is one of the most critical factors for successful inclusion. This worry about making friends is on a continuum: at the positive end there is their child being popular and well liked and having some special friends; at the negative end there is their child being teased or even bullied. Many parents are worried about bullying – not just the parents of children with physical difficulties. However, these parents believe their children may be taunted or teased because of their physical difficulties. Unfortunately, this is often the case. Bullying and making friends are interrelated. Bullying is more usual with children who are isolated and have few friends. The focus, therefore, in this chapter is ensuring that the child with a physical difficulty makes friends.

Preparing the class

In the same way, the head teacher or SENCO should prepare the staff before a child with a physical difficulty starts in a school, and the teacher should prepare the class. There is an argument that this singles out the child and draws attention to him being different. However, the child with a physical disability *is* different. The right thing to do is to acknowledge this as a way of moving forward. Quite how different he is will depend on the school. In some classes there may already be another child who uses a wheelchair. If this is the case, then being in a wheelchair is not being different. However, using a communication board may be. The purpose of preparing the class is to ease the transition into school, not to create additional problems. The age of the class will also affect how the class should be prepared but it can consist of information, activities and discussion. It may be helpful to have one of the child's parents join the teacher to talk to the class.

Information

Some of the information given in Chapter 2 can be shared. For example, if the child has cerebral palsy, the sort of information that can be shared about this condition might be:

- it is not an illness or disease; it can't be caught;
- it is something that you are born with;
- it means the brain has difficulty controlling parts of the body;
- it does not get worse;
- it is not painful and you do not die of it;
- a child with CP can be born into any family;
- sometimes children with CP have difficulty speaking but that does not mean they are stupid.

(Adapted from Scope (undated))

The children do not have to know all there is to know about the condition, but often two or three basic pieces of information will be very helpful.

Activities

There are also various activities that can be done with the class to help them understand what it is like to have a physical difficulty. The activities can be modified to the appropriate age of the child. Activities could include:

- Put on two pairs of thick gloves and then:
  - draw a circle;
  - write your name;
  - pick up a pencil or a coin.
- Put one of your hands in your pocket and then:
  - put on your shoes;
  - tie your shoelaces;

  – draw a straight line;
  – play a game of catch.
- Put both hands in your pockets and then:
  – draw a picture using a paintbrush in your mouth;
  – open the door;
  – drink a glass of water.
- Press your tongue to the bottom of your mouth and then:
  – tell someone your name;
  – tell someone what you did last night.

(Adapted from Scope *op. cit.*)

These activities should be fun. They should show the rest of the class that having a physical difficulty can be frustrating but that underneath there is still a little boy.

Discussion

One focus for the discussion can be on feelings. Following the activities the children can be asked how they felt about not being able to do things easily. Did they feel frustrated and annoyed? Did they feel like giving up? The second focus for the discussion is about what others could do to help. Would it be useful to have someone ask if they could help? How could they be helpful – picking up a pencil or opening a door? What would be helpful if you didn't understand what the other person was saying?

For older children this could be followed by a discussion on what is a 'normal' person. This could start with other types of special educational needs, for example children who are blind, but then lead to issues of difference, such as gender and race. The class can discuss going to school if you were the only boy, or girl, or were in a different country where you were the only white, black, or Asian child. Issues of size – if you were the biggest in the class, or the smallest – can be brought up. The teacher needs to focus the discussion on how difference is normal and how boring it would be if everyone was the same. Once again it is helpful to bring out how children feel if they are different.

Class action

The final part of the discussion should focus on how the class can help the new child settle in. Starting again with feelings, they can be asked to think about what it is like for the new child with a physical difficulty starting school. Each pupil can then be asked to think of one thing that they could do to help the new pupil. These types of discussion raise awareness of the social and emotional, as well as the practical, needs of the new child. They can orientate the class to how having a physical difficulty may well mean being different from the rest of the class, but how the child still has the same feelings and social needs (e.g. friendships) as everyone else.

This class preparation can be extended through the use of drama. Drama allows children to take on and try out different roles. They can enter into the world of another child and see what it feels like to be different or disabled. There are a number of programmes designed to facilitate the inclusion of children with disabilities (Marks 1997).

Acknowledging prejudice

The importance of preparing the class is also to combat any prejudice about the child with a physical difficulty. Prejudice is unjustified negative beliefs and feelings towards an individual or a group. It is a negative opinion formed about a child before he is known. Prejudice is a well-established phenomenon within human society and is prevalent towards a whole range of minority groups – including those with physical difficulties. Over the years there have been many theories about why prejudice occurs (Lynch 1987). Present thinking stresses its functional importance in protecting the individual's self-concept. Children (and adults) ascribe positive traits to the members of the group to which they belong. So boys ascribe positive characteristics to being boys, women ascribe positive characteristics to being a woman, black people ascribe positive characteristics to being black, and white to white. Prejudice is the positive comparison children make between their own characteristics (for example being a boy, black and able-bodied) and the characteristics of the other child (for example being a boy, black and disabled). Prejudice becomes a rational way for children to develop or maintain their self-esteem. It follows, therefore, that the lower the self-esteem of the pupil the more they are likely to feel prejudice towards other pupils.

Even preschool children see the child with a physical difficulty as different. This difference is often reinforced by the use of specialist equipment, for example a wheelchair or a standing frame (Diamond 1993). However, being different is often not, in itself, sufficient to produce prejudice. The differences have to be seen as somehow devaluing the child. So to take racial prejudice, how the different child in a class is reacted to depends on which country he comes from. The status of the country (economically or culturally) determines whether the child is discriminated against – the boy from Brazil is seen differently to the boy from Belize.

In our society, having a physical difficulty is often seen to devalue the child. Preschool children with a physical difficulty may not be chosen as playmates. Preschool children may think the child with a physical difficulty is not interested in playing or is not able to participate. More worryingly, there may be subtle messages given out that the child's physical difficulty somehow devalues him.

There are a number of factors that may reinforce this devaluing of children with physical difficulties.

Lack of role models

There are very few teachers who have physical difficulties, or for that matter other role models such as musicians or film stars. Many careers are effectively closed to people with physical difficulties. This is not because they could not undertake the job, sing or act or teach, but because society finds it difficult to accept that people with physical difficulties should do these things. People with physical disabilities find it extremely difficult to overcome many of the prejudices within society. There are exceptions – politicians such as David Blunkett and actors such as Nabil Shaban – but such obvious high-profile people with disabilities are few and far between. The lack of role models is being successfully challenged in some areas; in particular, the field of athletics, where the rise in popularity of the Para Olympics has been of enormous importance.

The teacher can tackle the lack of role models by ensuring that the materials used in the school are sensitive to disabled stereotypes. A well-known example of this is that of people with physical difficulties being bad or evil, for example Long John Silver. The portrayal of people with physical difficulties as having the same personal characteristics as everyone else – both good and bad, strong and weak – is an important message to give in the classroom.

Labelling

As soon as a child is labelled as being physically disabled it sets up certain reactions. The most obvious is that all people see is the label (the physical disability) rather than the child himself. The label 'having a physical disability' can be seen as the defining characteristic of the child. This book falls into this very trap by being entitled as being about children with 'physical disabilities'. It has tried to maintain some balance by showing that the effective inclusion of children with physical difficulties is in the hands of teachers, TAs, parents, other professionals and peers. Another problem is that generalisations can be made from labels. So all children with physical difficulties are believed to have difficulties with communication or toileting. This is particularly a problem if there is only limited inclusion of children with physical disabilities – one generalises from limited experience.

Adult influence

Children, particularly young children, look to adults to know how to respond to new situations. Teachers are particularly significant adults in children's lives, and their reactions to the child with a physical disability are particularly important (Marks 1997). It is known that teachers who are negative towards children with a disability are imitated by the children in their class (Parish *et al.* 1980). The teacher must be seen to be actively involved in teaching all the pupils in the class. If the child with a physical difficulty is seen as the responsibility of the TA this will reinforce a stereotype that the teacher does not teach these kinds of children. This book has stressed the importance of a team approach, which means that the teacher must be actively engaged in teaching the child with a physical disability. The children will watch how the teacher relates to the child with a physical difficulty and then use this as a guide to how they should develop friendships.

Psychological wellbeing

Many teachers recognise the difficulties that children with physical disabilities face, including prejudice from the able-bodied. The question is whether these difficulties affect the children psychologically. The able-bodied may believe that they will have emotional difficulties that relate to their actual physical difficulties: 'It must be terrible stuck in a wheelchair all day' or 'Imagine not being able to talk'. Sometimes it is related to social issues or making friends: 'Oh, but you couldn't have a normal relationship'. Such views have been reinforced over the years by many professionals who believe that children with physical difficulties are likely to have psychological and emotional problems (see, for example, Molnar 1992).

Able-bodied perception

One of the issues is that the able-bodied have particular difficulties in making sense of the experiences of the physically disabled. For the able-bodied, the body acts smoothly, without the need to think. In fact, thinking about the body, e.g. having a pain or ache, means something is not quite right. So, becoming conscious of our body can be anxiety-provoking. Having something wrong with the body can lead to death. So the able-bodied may find it quite difficult to be confronted on a daily basis by someone who has physical difficulties. In the same way many people feel uncomfortable about being surrounded by very old people as this also is a reminder that we are all mortal.

The point to remember is that though the able-bodied may have this difficulty, the child with a physical disability may not. This negative feedback the child with physical difficulties gets from the able-bodied is a well-known phenomenon. It can start at birth, with the child surrounded by people speaking about him as if there was something wrong (Scope 1994). The message, consciously or unconsciously, is given that a part of him is bad or crippled and needs to be mended. It is believed that such continuous negative perceptions will ultimately damage the child psychologically and lower his self-esteem.

Self-esteem

Self-esteem is about how the child values himself. Harter (1988) has shown that self-esteem is made up of a number of separate dimensions or domains. The two most important for all children are physical appearance and social acceptance. There would, then, appear to be particular issues surrounding self-esteem for children with physical difficulties. However, there are two sets of factors that affect self-esteem: the competency the child thinks he has on a particular domain – 'perceived competence'; and the importance of that domain to the child – his 'pretensions'. It is the discrepancy between a child's perceived competencies and his pretensions that causes high or low self-esteem. So a child who really wants to be a footballer but who is not captain of his school's football team may have a low self-esteem in this area. Vice versa, a child who attaches no importance to football but who scores a goal in the playground kick around may have very high self-esteem.

The child's self-esteem is developed through how he is treated by others – the 'looking-glass' effect. Friends who are positive towards the child will increase his self-esteem – he will see himself reflected in their positive comments. This is one of the reasons why having friends is so important. However, self-esteem is not a direct reflection of the feedback a child receives. In other words, the child can distort the 'looking-glass' through his beliefs about the person who is giving him the information. That person must have credibility in the child's eyes if his/her message is to have validity.

The self-esteem of children with a physical disability

Do children with physical difficulties have lower self-esteem than their able-bodied peers? Early research did support the view that children with a physical difficulty view themselves more negatively than do their able-bodied peers (Richardson *et al.* 1964). However, in the last few decades that view has changed. It is now recognised that the severity of the physical difficulty does not appear to affect self-esteem (Varni *et al.* 1989; Resnick and Hutton 1987). In other words, children with more severe physical difficulties do not have a lower self-esteem than children with more minor physical difficulties. More specifically, children with physical difficulties (in this research spina bifida) do not rate their physical appearance lower than their able-bodied peers (Appleton *et al.* 1994), though they did recognise that they were less competent as athletes.

Gender may have an influence on self-esteem when children are older. Adolescent girls with cerebral palsy have significantly lower social and physical self-esteem than boys with CP. These gender differences should not overshadow the view that, generally, children with physical difficulties do not have lower self-esteem than their able-bodied peers.

Specific issues for children with mild physical difficulties

One of the interesting findings from the above studies is that there is no connection between the severity of a physical disability and self-esteem. In fact, the opposite may be true, that children with more mild physical difficulties may have more psychological and emotional difficulties. One of the reasons for this is that these difficulties are more invisible; the focus is usually on the child's obvious physical problem, his physical mobility or communication difficulties. However, children with physical difficulties may have a whole range of more subtle needs. Children with hemiplegia are one such group of children who have particular invisible emotional needs. Their physical difficulties are usually quite minor with, maybe, some difficulties in walking and coordinating. However, many of these children have emotional or behavioural difficulties and difficulties with relationships (Goodman 1997). Children with hemiplegia often are non-compliant, anxious and have difficulties with their attention span. These difficulties can cause substantial distress for the child and disruption for teachers in the classroom.

The non-compliance of some children with hemiplegia can be seen in reluctance to go along with adults' requests. It is the sort of behaviour one expects from a 'terrible two'. It is, of course, a particular difficulty in a class of 30 five-year-olds. This irritability and non-compliance leads to conflict and the child can easily lose his temper. However, Goodman (*op. cit.*) suggests that it should be recognised that children with hemiplegia have a 'low boiling point'. In other words, they over-react and get emotionally wound-up in situations that would not make other children angry or anxious. Children with hemiplegia are not deliberately aggressive in an antisocial way; instead they are reactive aggressive and emotionally over-sensitive. They also have difficulties with friendships.

Most children with hemiplegia do have friends. However, they find it difficult to make reciprocal friends. They are also likely to be teased or bullied. These difficulties may be to do with a range of the above reasons. It may be that their irritability and low boiling point means it is easy to get a reaction out of them. It may also be that children with hemiplegia have difficulties understanding other people's perspectives, and this contributes to their emotional and social immaturity.

Children with hemiplegia can be helped with these problems. A particularly useful source of information in this country is Hemi-Help, a parents' organisation. Hemi-Help produces newsletters and information sheets on a whole range of issues, including education. The first thing to understand is that these difficulties – irritability, non-compliance and short attention span – are a part of the problems associated with the hemiplegia. It is not because of family or classroom factors. However, it is important that the teacher and parents work together to see how family and classroom factors can be modified to make life better for these children.

Resilience

The general picture that emerges from the above contradicts the view that children with a physical disability inevitably, or even usually, have more psychological problems or a lower self-esteem than their able-bodied peers. Instead, the child with a physical disability is likely to be psychologically well adjusted and possess a high self-esteem. One way of explaining this is the distinction between the individual and social model outlined in Chapter 3. One aspect of the individual model is to see the physically disabled child as grieving a loss (Swain *et al.* 1993). However, the social model of disability views the main problem as the attitude of others and a lack of resources. This social model of disability means the child with physical difficulties may see any problems as residing outside himself, in peers, teachers and the social world. In fact, having a physical disability may provide psychological strength and motivation rather than being psychologically damaging, as the child recognises his uniqueness (Crocker and Major 1989).

This is not to deny the psychological difficulties that some children with physical difficulties have. Girls may be a more vulnerable group, as may children with milder physical difficulties. Teachers and TAs can do most to influence social support in the classroom. In particular, they have a key role in the development of friendships with peers.

Frames of friendship

Six frames of friendship can be used to think about the friendship patterns of children with physical difficulties (Meyer 2001). These are all natural forms of friendship for all children – disabled and able-bodied. All are appropriate in certain circumstances and there should be a balance between them.

Ghost or guest

If the child is seen as a guest, he may initially get a lot of attention. However, if things get difficult he is either ignored (like a ghost) or asked to leave. Being a visitor implies that he does not really belong, but as long as he is here then he will be treated well. The child may sit like an invisible presence at the back of the class. Peers do not interact with him or involve him in their activities. Being a ghost or guest is sometimes a good thing. It is good that the child with a physical disability can be ignored – as it can for all children. The problem is when this is the *only* way he is treated for the whole of the school day.

Inclusion child

The second frame of reference has, again, positive and negative features. Generally, both parents and teachers want the child with a physical difficulty to be treated differently and his special needs to be acknowledged. This may be reinforced by needing provision outside the classroom, thus ensuring that the child is seen and treated differently. Depending on how the programme is managed this may make the child seem different to his peers, and a different kind of friendship occurs. The child can be seen as someone who is needy, like a younger sibling – someone to be babied and talked down to.

'I'll help'

In this frame the child is seen by his peers as someone who needs help. Many parents find that peer help, often known as 'buddying', is one of the very real benefits of inclusion. Though friendship is about giving help there should be an expectation that this is mutual. This is not to deny the very real difficulties that some children with physical difficulties may have with helping. However, the barrier to helping should be about the actual difficulties the child has and not the attitude of his friends.

Just another child

In one way, this is the most inclusive. The child is treated just like all the other pupils.

Regular friend

A regular friend is someone who will happily play with the child, sit beside him at lunchtime and share activities in the classroom. Regular friends are likely to choose each other to be on a team, or invite each other to a large party, but not a birthday treat for three.

Best friend

A best friend is often described as a friend for life. A best friend is someone to whom the child turns when he has a problem or some exciting news. Best friends want to spend time playing together at school and at each other's homes.

These six frames of friendship all contribute to well-balanced relationships. Having a best friend and regular friends is the basis for the child's socialisation. In certain situations the child may be a guest. It is also right to get help at times from others, and, of course, to give help. The child with physical difficulties is different, and this should be acknowledged. Part of this acknowledgement can be to think about whether having a special friend – a 'buddy' – would be useful.

The use of special friends

Children with physical difficulties may not develop friendships with their peers spontaneously (Strully and Strully 1989). The development of special friends, or 'buddies', is often a helpful starting point to facilitate such friendships. Buddies are children who are identified to help the child with a physical difficulty. They are used extensively in the States to help the inclusion of children. Buddy systems can be, initially, quite formal, where children are identified to do particular tasks – for example help the child to the lunch hall. However, it is the informal friendship role that is most important. This is where the buddy becomes responsive to the social and emotional needs of the child. The buddy has a role not only in the classroom but also at playtime. In fact, it is at playtime that buddies can come into their own as the teacher and TA take a back seat.

For children with difficulties in communicating it is very helpful to develop buddies who are interested in understanding the child and who will take the time to sit and communicate. For this to be successful the buddy needs to be taught quite explicitly how the communication system works and even to be part of some paired work with the child.

Buddies are an important aspect of social inclusion but they are not without their difficulties. It is important that the child is not simply identified as one needing help – the 'I'll help' relationship. This simply creates a dependency relationship which is not particularly healthy. The buddy should have similar interests and experiences to the child, as friendships depend on shared interests. The child's peers need to know what his interests are. The allocation of a buddy needs to take into account mutual interests, rather than simply seeing who would be willing to help. This then moves the role of the buddy from simply helping the child to that of friendship. Children may be taught some of the values of friendships, such as loyalty and interest in others, as the basis for development of friendships across the classroom.

Friendship patterns

As a regular part of a class activity children can be asked to identify their friends. This, for example, can be done termly so that as friendships develop and change they can be monitored. This type of analysis is called sociometry and was developed to understand how people relate to each other.

Instructions
Tell the class that you are planning for them to work in groups on a big painting next month. Ask them to select three other children with whom they would like to work and write their names on a piece of paper. If they are too young to write they could come up and tell the teacher, one at a time. Ask them to identify (underline) the one name they would most like to work with. They should do this on their own without discussing it with each other.

Drawing the sociogram
This sociogram not only identifies each pupil's best friend (the underlined name), it also identifies their regular friends. A diagram can be drawn to represent the friendship patterns (see Figure 6.1). A circle represents each child. Children who choose each other are drawn close together, with the direction of the arrow indicating who has done the choosing. The heavy arrow indicates the child's best friend.

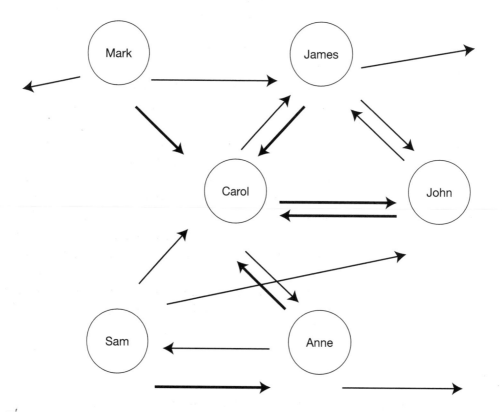

Figure 6.1 . Sociogram of friendships

Analysis

The information in Figure 6.1 shows that Carol is very popular with her peers. She is chosen by four of them as their best friend, and Sam also chooses her. John and James form a little clique with her, but she also has a friendship with Anne who is ignored by the other two. Sam and, particularly, Mark seem to be quite isolated. Mark has no reciprocal relationships at all and Sam only has one with Anne.

This simple analysis can begin to show friendship patterns in the classroom. Who is the child with a physical difficulty? If it is Carol, then there is no need to worry, as she has already established a network of friends. If, however, it is Mark, then one can see how he is already becoming isolated in the class. When thinking about a buddy for Mark the starting point would be Carol or James – children that he had picked. However, it would also be worth considering whether one of the others in this group – Sam or Anne – might also make a good buddy, provided they share common interests.

The teacher can encourage friendships in a variety of ways. One of the most effective ways is by ensuring physical proximity and interaction through classroom groupings.

Classroom groupings for friendships

One important way the teacher fosters friendship is through the grouping of pupils in the classroom. At the most fundamental level the question is, 'Where will the pupil with a physical disability sit in the classroom?' There are some practical issues here depending, for example, on whether the pupil has special seating or needs a certain amount of space to manoeuvre his wheelchair. There are also psychological issues; it may be easier to place him at the side or the back, but will this really promote inclusion or help him to make friends? One helpful strategy is to think about how the rest of the class are placed. Do they move tables every half-term? If the answer is 'yes', then so should the child with a physical disability. Can they choose whom they sit near? Then so should he. If they are grouped differently for different activities, then so should the child who has a physical difficulty. In a very explicit way the placement of the child in the classroom space can be seen to mirror the feelings of inclusion. However, in the same way as the teacher may wish to place a child in particular proximity to another child, so they may wish to move the child with physical difficulties to place him beside a potential friend or buddy. The sociometric analysis provides information on how to group children together. It is this information that the teacher can use to actively foster friendship. Being in close proximity has been shown to be an important strategy to both reduce prejudice and increase friendship (Stainback and Stainback 1990).

Learning that promotes friendships

Ideally, the child with a physical difficulty is placed in the class near to his friends. Where and how he is placed affects the type of learning in which he can participate. A distinction can be made between three types of learning:

- competitive – where children work to do better than their peers;
- individual – where children work on their own; and
- cooperative – where there is a positive interdependence between children.

It is the last two of these types of learning which are particularly important for the child with a physical difficulty. The focus for the child will often be on individual learning. This is reinforced by the individual nature of their physical management and, probably, their communication programme. It is also reinforced by the TA who may feel that she has to work individually with the child. Thus the child may spend most of his time working by himself, sometimes on an individualised curriculum. Some individual learning is important for the child; however, if this is the *only* type of learning he has access to then his learning opportunities will be severely restricted.

Cooperative learning strategies

In contrast to individual learning, cooperative learning assumes that pupils have to work together to undertake a task or activity (Johnson and Johnson 1987). An example of cooperative learning is painting a wall mural where all the children contribute. Another example is writing about the sea, where all the children contribute words that will be used. Cooperative learning means that the children have to help and assist each other to learn.

Four basic cooperative learning strategies can be used: student team learning; jigsaw; learning together; and group investigations.

Student team learning is when a group of children work together to learn new materials. So, for example, a group of children (including the one with a physical difficulty) work together to learn the sight vocabulary for a new book. Group members help each other to learn and correct the mistakes of each other. Afterwards, each child can be tested to see if s/he knows the words.

Jigsaw is a very popular cooperative learning strategy. The class is divided into groups and each group member is given different information to understand. Children who are studying the same information meet as a small, expert group. They make sure that they understand it and then return to their own group to explain it to the rest of the group, supplemented by the knowledge and understanding gained from working in the expert group. So the class could be learning about the Romans. The material is divided into five areas: home life; the army; the government system; conquests; entertainment (gladiators). The class is divided into groups of five. One member from each group joins to form an expert group, for example on the army. This expert group learns as much as it can about the army. Each member returns to their original group and shares what they have learnt with the others. Each group could then produce a mural showing what life was like in Roman times.

Learning together revolves around the group obtaining only one copy of the material to be studied and then having to complete a single project. This means that they have to work together to complete the task. Different members of the group can take different parts of the work. The child with a physical disability can be given a particular part that suits his own skills.

Group investigation is a very open-ended, problem-solving type of strategy. It requires the group of children to decide what and how they are going to learn and how they are going to communicate back to the class what they have learnt. So at the end of the year each group could be asked to do a group investigation of what they have learnt in history. One group could write a folder on the Roman army, one could dress up and march like the army, and another could construct a gladiatorial arena.

These types of cooperative learning were not developed specifically for children with physical disabilities. They are, however, good examples of how a child can be included within a class group. The point of all these methods is that they allow the teacher to use the forces inherent in a small group to foster not only learning but also friendships. The tasks are structured so that the children feel that they are all in it together. They need to help each other in order for the tasks to be completed successfully. The benefits for class learning are twofold. They are a very good way of ensuring that the children have a really good understanding of a particular area. For example, in Jigsaw the children have to really understand their material to feed it back to the others. In addition, the children have to learn to work together. The children have to develop basic interpersonal skills, such as effective communication, as well as the respect and genuineness that leads to trust and friendship between children. Finally, of course, these types of cooperative learning allow the child with a physical difficulty and his peers to work together. Such work acknowledges what the child can contribute to the learning process as well as being of enormous psychological benefit for inclusion.

Playground grouping for friendship

The development of friendships can happen in the classroom. However, playtime and lunch-break are two other obvious times when friendships can develop. There are, however, a number of reasons why playtime may not be used by the child with a physical difficulty to develop friendships:

- there may be limited active intervention by teachers and TAs, as it is seen as free playtime (and they also need their break);
- the unstructured, fast-moving nature of interactions in the playground are difficult for children with physical disabilities;
- they may not be able to access all the playground (there may be steps to some areas); and
- they may have limited experience of playing 'outdoor games'.

(Adapted from Nabors *et al.* 2001)

It is important to overcome these barriers so that playtime can take its proper place as an integral part of the child's education. There are a number of ways to do this. The playground may need to be structurally adapted to ensure it is accessible. Adaptations to the environment are one way of ensuring that there is no area of the playground that is off-limits for children with physical difficulties. Such changes are imperative now with the introduction of the Special Educational Needs and Disability Act (DfES 2001b) and should be included in the school's Accessibility Plan (see Chapter 8). A related, but separate, issue is for children who require a wheelchair for mobility. They will need an outdoor wheelchair to access the playground. The NHS does not automatically provide one. The school needs to demonstrate its commitment to seeing playtime as fundamental to the child's learning. In this way the argument can be made during the Statementing procedure that the child requires an outdoor wheelchair as part of the Provision to meet his Needs (see Chapter 7).

In addition to issues of accessibility, structural changes can be undertaken. In particular, the development of play centres is a way of structuring playtime so that social interaction is more likely to occur (see Nabors *et al. op. cit.*). The play centres can mirror the types of activity centres created in most nursery and infant classrooms. For example, a 'shop' could include costumes to wear, goods to sell and money to spend. A shop can only be fun if children play together. A sand centre, with rakes, buckets and spades, would allow a child in a wheelchair to play alongside his peers. Such centres also provide a natural opportunity for teachers to be involved with the children. This can be at the level of active involvement in modelling play or providing verbal encouragement to extend or develop activities.

It is important to design centres that encourage cooperative rather than individual play. So it has been found that individual or solitary play is encouraged by books, art materials and puzzles. On the other hand, cooperative play is encouraged by dressing-up clothes, puppets, toy cars and lorries, and balls (Martin *et al.* 1991). It is helpful if these play centres can be enclosed. This slows down the pace of the playtime and moves those children who want to play in a centre away from the direct bustle of the playground. Such action is not trying to ghettoise the child's playtime, it is simply trying to offer an alternative structure that may be more fun for them.

Cooperative play in the playground

Teachers can build on these structural changes by taking an active part in facilitating the development of cooperative play. Play centres provide a vehicle to allow this to happen. In the same way that the teacher can encourage cooperative learning in the classroom, they can also encourage cooperative play at playtime. It is a way of building relationships as well as about teaching children how to cooperate. Cooperation on the playground can be facilitated by the following techniques:

- **group affection activities**: Develop songs and games that show affection: 'If you're happy and you know it hug a friend'.
- **cooperative activities**: These are activities that children have to work at together to solve. For example, staying on a pretend island while making the island smaller and smaller. The children have to learn to hold onto each other.
- **stories**: The teacher develops a story like going shopping, or sailing a pirate ship. The children take various parts and have to act it out. The teacher can be the audience.
- **team activities**: Teams can be organised to build sandcastles, collect leaves or make a garden.
- **prompting**: The teacher prompts the children to interact with each other.

All the above call for direct intervention by the teacher. In addition there are many opportunities for what can be described as incidental teaching at playtime. This is when something happens naturally that the teacher can extend or reinforce. For example, the teacher sees two children trying to help the child with a physical disability move to the sand area. The teacher can join them and ask what they are going to build together. In this way the teacher simply reinforces and extends what the children are already doing.

The greatest barrier to making playtime more successful for the child with a physical difficulty is accepting that it may not be a free playtime for them. There is a belief that cooperative interactions may occur naturally if children are just allowed to play by themselves. For the child with a physical difficulty this may not be initially viable. The child may have difficulty initiating and sustaining interactions with his peers. He may have difficulty in actually joining in activities and keeping up with the movement in a fast-moving environment. For these reasons the teacher's direct facilitation of play is likely to be required if friendships are to be encouraged.

Summary

In this chapter the importance of developing friendships has been explored. In particular, it has emphasised how the teacher can

- develop an induction programme for the class;
- recognise possible sources of prejudice against the child with physical difficulty;
- understand the psychological and emotional wellbeing of the child;
- recognise different types of friendship in the class;
- promote cooperative learning in the classroom; and
- promote cooperative learning in the playground.

CHAPTER 7

Needs and Provision

The Statement

The Special Educational Needs Code of Practice (DfES 2001a) confirms that the Statement is the document which sets out the child's Special Educational Needs (SEN) and the Provision that he requires. Though children with a mild physical difficulty may not have a Statement, most children with more severe difficulties will have one. This is to protect their rights by ensuring that both their Needs are accurately identified and the Provision to meet those Needs is provided. The statementing process is not only about the initial assessment but also about the annual Statutory Reviews through which progress is reviewed and targets are set for the next year. This chapter is designed to help ensure statementing helps the child with a physical difficulty.

The importance of the Statement

There is considerable debate at the moment about the importance of the Statement. The Audit Commission's (2002) report *Statutory Assessments and Statements of Special Educational Needs* highlights a number of these issues:

- the times and cost of producing Statements;
- the usefulness of the information they contain;
- the allocation of resources as detailed in the Statement; and
- the assurance that the Needs specified in the Statement are being met.

These are problematic for all children with SEN, not simply those with physical difficulties. All too often the Statement is simply a document that sits in the school's office. Many teachers feel that it has little relevance to what actually happens in their classroom. However, the Statement can be a very valuable tool. It carries with it certain rights for the child and responsibilities for the professionals. It is best seen as a document that underpins the child's rights to have his needs identified and met. Once in place it can then be used as a guideline for what should be happening for this child. The focus in this chapter is ensuring that the child has an accurate Statement that supports his rights to inclusion. In this regard teachers are seen as championing inclusion through advocacy.

The importance of advocacy

Advocating for the child's rights is an important part of inclusion. Advocacy can be contrasted with negotiation as a way of resolving problems. Negotiation is the way that teachers usually resolve problems when working with professionals, parents and other teachers. Negotiation is useful when people have different views, all of which have some validity. Advocacy, on the other hand, is useful when there is a clear structure which gives clear rights to a particular individual. When one is short-changed in a shop or sold faulty goods one does not negotiate over the situation. One has certain consumer rights which should be advocated for. In a similar way, advocacy is useful when resolving issues to do with Statements. The Statementing procedure is designed to ensure that the child's Special Educational Needs are specified and that the school has the resources to meet those Needs. There is detailed guidance contained in the Code of Practice about how this should be undertaken. It is disastrous to start negotiating over a child's rights, as detailed in the Code of Practice, when they should be advocated for.

Everyone advocates at some time or another. Teachers are not formal advocates. They are, though, informal advocates in so far as advocacy is basically about 'Speaking up for yourself or for another person, to secure rights, meet needs or support people to make informed choices' (Lovell 2001).

For whom do teachers advocate?

Advocacy for the child with a physical difficulty not only means speaking up for him but also empowering him to speak up for himself. This is one of the major changes of the Revised Code of Practice which emphasises the importance of the views of the child being sought and listened to.

The teacher may also, at times, be advocating on behalf of the parents. Another key aspect of the Revised Code of Practice is on working in partnership with parents. It is, though, important to recognise that at times there may be differences between the parents' and the child's views.

However, teachers are not independent advocates. They are employed by the school and have responsibilities to it. When they advocate for the child they are also advocating for the other children in the class, their parents and the school as an organisation. They are ensuring that the child with physical difficulties' needs are identified and met. They are advocating for their rights as teachers to be respected by ensuring that the Statement is safeguarded.

At the Annual Review, or at other times during the statementing process, it is often helpful for the teacher or the TA to clearly decide which one of them will take up the role of advocating for the child. For example, the TA can become the child's advocate, putting forward his point of view while the teacher takes a broader view of the issues. In reality, 90 per cent of the time, these two roles overlap. However, this device allows the TA to be clear that they are speaking for the child and not for themselves in the Review.

Bearing this split in roles in mind, there are a number of key principle to which the child's advocate should adhere:

- **Independence** – the advocate must feel that her first loyalty is to the child when advocating for him, not to the school or LEA.
- **Impartiality** – the role of the advocate is to speak on behalf of the child, and not to give her own view.
- **Non-judgemental** – the role of the advocate is not to make judgements about what the child says and whether it is right or not.
- **Enabling** – the role of the advocate is to give the child information about what is happening.
- **Choice** – the child should be given the choice about whom he wants as an advocate – TA, teacher, SENCO or someone outside the school.
- **Confidentiality** – the child should be asked if he is happy for all he says to be shared (subject to the law of the land).
- **Equal opportunities** – the advocate should be sensitive to any cultural or racial differences between herself and the child.
- **Clarity** – the role of the advocate should be extremely clear to the child.

(Adapted from Lovell 2001)

Should the child be statemented?

The Audit Commission (2002) has highlighted the debate on whether children should be statemented. Different LEAs have different positions on this question but many are seeking to reduce the number of children who are statemented. Statementing is seen as a long and expensive process. One view is that it would be more helpful to delegate budgets to schools so that they could arrange their own support. This would eliminate the need for a Statement

However, parents usually see Statements as safeguarding the support their children need in school. Teachers are often in the middle of these two positions. They may think that the only way to get support for a child is to have him statemented. On the other hand, they often do not find the Statement useful and would prefer the money to be delegated.

This book takes the position that statementing, and the Review of the Statement, is a process that safeguards the rights of the child. If the school, and other agencies, could make the process work to the satisfaction of parents, without the need for statementing, then the Statement itself is unimportant. What is important is a clear, accountable process showing how the child is being helped to progress by the provision provided. This chapter provides strategies to ensure pupils, parents and the professionals are clear about what is being provided to meet which needs.

Does the child have Special Educational Needs?

The law says that a child has Special Educational Needs if he has learning difficulties which require specific help, known as Special Educational Provision.

The child has a learning difficulty if he:

(a) has a disability which makes it difficult to use the normal educational facilities in the area; and/or
(b) finds it much harder to learn than most children of the same age.

It is important to remember that he does not *also* have to find it harder to learn, that is be a slower learner, than most children of the same age. If the child has a sensory or physical disability and finds it difficult to use the normal educational facilities in the school then he can be considered to have a learning difficulty. If he has a learning difficulty which requires Special Educational Provision, then he has Special Educational Needs and should have a Statement.

The above definitions make it clear that it is not simply the severity of the child's physical difficulty but rather the educational facilities which are normally available that decide whether the child should have a Statement. For example, a child in a school without a TA or physiotherapy support might require a Statement. A child with the same level of physical difficulties, but with these resources already in place, might well not require a Statement.

How the teacher can give the child a voice

The assessment for statementing takes the form of gathering **Advice** from a range of people. Central to this process are the views of the child. One of the fundamental principles of the Code of Practice is that the views of the child should be sought and taken into account. This requires bringing together a number of areas. First and foremost, it is about building a relationship with the child and developing his communication skills as described in Chapter 5. This may be particularly difficult with a very young child. Secondly, it means taking up the role of the advocate as described earlier in this chapter. In other words one role of the teacher, or TA, is to ensure the child's views are represented within the assessment process.

In addition, if the child's (or parents') first language is not English, the LEA should assist the school to obtain the help of bilingual staff to ensure the child (and parents) is able to express his views. The child's views should be known in a number of areas. Quite how the questions are asked will depend on the age of the child.

1. Curriculum

E.g.:

- What do you most like doing in school?
- What do you least like doing in school?
- Which things would you like more help with?
- What is the most important thing to learn in school?

2. Teaching

E.g.:

- Which teachers (adults) do you like to work with?
- How do they help you?
- Which teachers (adults) do you not like to work with?
- What do teachers (adults) do to make learning fun?

3. Peers

E.g.:

- Who are your best friends?
- Which pupil do you most like to sit near?
- Which pupils do you not like to be near?
- What do you do at playtime/break? Who do you play with?
- What would they like to do at playtime/break?

4. School

E.g.:

- Do you like the school?
- Are there any difficulties getting to school?
- Are there any difficulties getting around school (including toileting)?
- How could things be improved?
- Are you ever worried or frightened in school?

Empowerment

Obtaining the child's views is important for the teacher in helping to understand him. It also empowers the child by showing him that his views are sought and taken into account. The United Nations Convention on the Rights of the Child recognises that children have a right to obtain and make known information, to express an opinion and to have that opinion taken into account in any matter or procedure affecting them. By making it clear at an early age that the child has the right to a voice, it makes it increasingly easier for him, as he grows older, to take ownership of his own life. In the first few years this may not be clear, but gradually the child will learn to take a more active role in his own reviews and be able to advocate for himself. Advocacy and empowerment should not be seen as a negative process. Instead, in the long run, they help to create a partnership where the child takes a much more active role in his own education.

Teachers can help empower children with physical difficulties by ensuring that the child:

- has control and choice;
- develops an identity;
- participates through consultation;
- has access to technology;
- has access to information; and
- has access to resources.

For pupils with a physical difficulty independence is an important outcome of empowerment. Some children with physical disabilities may never become completely physically independent. However, if they are empowered they can be independent. No-one, not even the able-bodied, is completely independent. Everyone relies on others for their 'independent' living. The aim, through empowerment, is independent education where the child is able to make decisions and participate fully in the school. Listening to the child is therefore the first and most crucial part of the assessment process.

Collaborative Advice

As well as the views of the child, the Statement is based on written

- parental Advice;
- educational Advice;
- medical Advice;
- psychological Advice; and
- social services Advice.

The LEA will also get Advice from anyone else whom the parents request. The Advice that is collected should form an accurate and comprehensive picture of the child.

Chapter 4 examines how the effective education of a child with a physical difficulty depends on transdisciplinary teamwork. Three aspects of transdisciplinary teamwork were highlighted:

- professionals work with the child together;
- meetings share knowledge, collaboratively set goals and develop new perspectives; and
- single set of records is kept and written collaboratively.

If Advice for a Statement is requested when the child is already in nursery or school, it can be completed in a transdisciplinary way. In other words, the secondary team of people working with the child produce the Advice collectively. To do this they have to work together to assess the child's SEN. They then need to collaboratively set objectives and to agree on what provision is required.

It may not be possible to produce one collaboratively written report, but the Advice from the different professionals, for example the teacher, psychologist and physiotherapist, should fit together. There needs to be agreement about which professional writes about which area. This means that one person writes about the child's physical difficulties. This, for example, could be the physiotherapist, but she would include in her report the views of the other professionals. The teacher might focus her report on accessing the curriculum but this would be tied to the speech and language therapist's analysis of the child's development of language through an AAC system.

The Statement has to follow a certain format. Each part of the Statement should contain specific information. The teacher should provide Advice in the same format. This ensures that the Advice can be clearly related to the final Statement.

The Statement format is:

1. Background information
2. The Special Educational Needs
3. The Provision to meet these Needs
    3.1. Objectives
    3.2. Provision to meet Needs and objectives
    3.3. Monitoring
4. Placement.

The special educational needs

The first step is to ensure that all the child's Special Educational Needs are identified. These should be specified in the Statement in Part 2: Special Educational Needs. This part can cause a lot of difficulties. The key thing to remember is that it should be a description of all the child's Special Educational Needs. This is a

Checklist for Teachers: Special Educational Needs

1. Does the child have a physical difficulty?

Sub-area	Yes	No	Don't know	Comments
Mobility				
Head control				
Sitting				
Using hands				

2. Does the child have visual difficulties?

Sub-area	Yes	No	Don't know	Comments
Visual input				
Visual processing				

3. Does the child have auditory difficulties?

Sub-area	Yes	No	Don't know	Comments
Conductive				
Sensorineural				

4. Does the child have any medical difficulties?

Sub-area	Yes	No	Don't know	Comments
Epilepsy				
Other (specify)				

5. Does the child have difficulties with skills of independent living?

Sub-area	Yes	No	Don't know	Comments
Dressing				
Undressing				
Mealtimes				
Toileting				

6. Does the child have difficulties with communication?

Sub-area	Yes	No	Don't know	Comments
Interactional skills				
Speech				
Comprehension				

7. Does the child have learning difficulties?

Sub-area	Yes	No	Don't know	Comments
In all subjects				
In specific areas Reading				
Mathematics				
Writing				

8. Does the child have social, emotional or behavioural difficulties?

Sub-area	Yes	No	Don't know	Comments
Relationship with adults				
Relationship with peers				
Self-esteem				

Table 7.1   Checklist for teachers: Special Educational Needs

description of those areas where he has a learning difficulty, i.e. a significantly greater difficulty in learning than other children or a disability which prevents him from making use of the educational facilities available in the school.

In other words it is a description of the problem areas where the child needs to develop, not the resources (or aids or equipment) that he needs. This book has covered many of the main areas that the teacher may be concerned about. It is worthwhile checking whether the child has needs in any of eight areas (Table 7.1).

The purpose of this is to provide an initial check to see that these areas have been covered. The clearer the Special Educational Needs are described in Part 2 of the

Statement the better. The Statement should include a description of the child's current functioning – what he can do. These can be taken from the above checklist. It should not contain all the background and developmental details which should be in the Advice. If the child has a significant difficulty in any of these eight areas it should be detailed in the Advice and on the Statement. In addition, the sub-area should be specified if the Statement is to be helpful to the school. If an area of difficulty has been omitted from the Statement it is important that it is not ignored. The Statement may need to be rewritten to ensure that it is included.

The special needs can be set out in a variety of ways. One example is given in Figure 7.1.

Special Education Provision

As well as identifying SENs, the Statement also has to identify what Provision is required to meet these needs. This is Part 3: Special Education Provision of the Statement. LEAs write Statements in different ways. However, the Revised Code of Practice makes it quite clear what Part 3 should contain. It should contain details of the Provision, that is the resources, required to meet the Special Educational Needs described in Part 2. That is why it is so important to ensure that all Needs are detailed in Part 2. If the areas of difficulty have not been accurately described then it is likely that the Provision will also not be accurate.

Jim is a six-year-old little boy. He is a happy little boy and especially likes the company of other young children of his own age. He is able to use some single words to name objects but has difficulties putting two-word phrases together. He uses a communication board and seems to understand at an age-appropriate level. He enjoys most aspects of the National Curriculum but is having particular difficulties with learning to read. He has good hand control and is learning to copy words. He is able to change his position and pull himself upright using furniture. He is able to attend to his own toilet and feeding needs once he is in the right place.

The evidence from the Physiotherapist, detailed in her advice, shows that Jim has difficulties with mobility around the classroom and school.

The evidence from the teacher, detailed in her advice, shows that Jim has visual-perceptual difficulties, which is affecting the development of his reading and access to other curriculum areas.

The evidence from the Speech and Language Therapist, detailed in her advice, shows that Jim has a difficulty with his expressive language.

The evidence from the parents, set out in their advice, supports these special educational needs.

There are no significant differences or contradictions in the submitted advice when specifying Jim's needs.

Figure 7.1 Example Part 2: Special Educational Needs

Part 3 is divided into 3 sections:

- Objectives;
- Educational Provision to meet Needs and objectives; and
- Monitoring.

Objectives

Section 1 should specify the main educational and developmental objectives which should be achieved by the Special Educational Provision. These are meant to be the long-term objectives in terms of what the child is expected to achieve over the duration of the Statement (see, for example, Figure 7.2).

This, of course, can be very difficult. If the child is having a Statement prepared when he is 3 or 4, it is very difficult to look ahead to the future to predict how he will develop over the next ten years. However, the purpose of setting objectives in the Statement is just this – to ensure that the professionals involved in working with the child have a clear view of what they are aiming to achieve. These objectives can be developed from the vision or dream that is part of the MAPS process (see Chapter 3). By having this clear view it is more likely that the child will achieve it.

Mobility

1. To be independently mobile within the classroom.

2. To be independently mobile with an electric wheelchair in the community.

Gross motor

1. To be able to position himself independently.

2. To be able to maintain trunk and head control for extended periods.

Cognitive

1. To be working at level 2 of the National Curriculum for English, Mathematics and Science.

Language

1. To use augmentative communication to communicate effectively with his peers and teachers.

Figure 7.2 Example Part 3 Section 1: Objectives

The objectives can be changed at the Statutory Review if they are achieved or if it is decided that other objectives are more important.

Setting targets collaboratively

Once the objectives are set, these need to be divided into smaller yearly targets. These targets can be set at the Annual Review. The targets do not have to be specified on the Statement and should be seen as the steps to obtain each objective.

There may, of course, be differences between professionals and between parents and professionals on what are the best targets for a child (Bailey 1987). People may disagree over either the targets or the strategy required to meet those targets. Underpinning these differences may be well be different values. One parent may take a social model of disability (see Chapter 3) and see the issues of inclusion really being about their child accessing the National Curriculum. They may not see the importance of the child learning to position himself this year. However, the class teacher may believe that a priority objective must be the child's ability to sit upright and that until this is achieved the educational curriculum comes second. These views, of course, may be the other way around. The point is that there is disagreement.

Setting targets and objectives collaboratively explicitly recognises the different perspectives of different people. By doing so it is much more likely that everyone 'buys into' the final agreed targets and shares the responsibility for them being reached.

Nominal group technique

Setting targets collaboratively can be done in a variety of ways. One helpful way is through the Nominal Group Technique. This is a way of ensuring everybody involved in the child has an opportunity to state their priorities. The steps are as follows:

- the objectives on the Statement are listed on a board or large sheet of paper;
- each member of the secondary team then writes on yellow post-its the three key targets that they want the child to achieve in the next year;
- these are then displayed underneath the appropriate objective;
- after everyone has written their three targets on the post-its they are discussed;
- people may want to modify their post-its or rewrite them in light of other people's comments;
- the targets can be further grouped together if they are very similar;
- under each objective the group then decides on the most appropriate target.

The problem is that there may be a long list of targets and it is still not clear what are the priorities. It is important to acknowledge that time is limited. This is not an issue about resources or support for the school; there are only a limited number of hours in a day and days in a year. Time spent on one target will limit time on another.

A helpful exercise in addressing the above issues is for each person to imagine that the child has 100 hours of direct input to meet his targets. This is divided into 60 hours for his priority target, 30 hours for the next most important and 10 hours for the third most important. How would this time be best used? What targets are the most critical? How should the time be divided between these targets? The point of the activity is not to map out the child's curriculum or timetable but rather for people to think through what they think is important for the child to achieve. What importance, in terms of how much of the 100 hours, would each person allocate to the different targets?

Doing this exercise helps the team feel and understand the frustration that they often will have. Choosing between targets when they all seem important or recognising that the heart-felt priority for one person is not the same for others is an important part of the process of planning the Provision in a way that will really make a difference for the child.

By setting targets collaboratively in this way a number of critical issues are addressed:

- recognising and acknowledging that people may have different values about what is important for the child;
- ensuring that everyone's view is heard and treated with respect;
- recognising that this child is part of a family who in the long term will have responsibility for his needs;
- acknowledging that the professionals have expertise through their training and experience and can see beyond the individual child; and
- achieving some sort of balance and synthesis of views so that everyone feels that their most important targets are incorporated.

Provision to meet Needs and objectives

The second section in Part 3 of the Statement should specify all the Educational Provision which is required to meet all the Needs (outlined in Part 2) and all the objectives which stem from these Needs. This means all the special help which the child should get. It does not matter if the Provision is paid for by the school, the LEA or the health authority; it should all be detailed.

The Provision must be specific, detailed and quantified in terms of the number of hours of teaching support or therapy, or the type of equipment required. This subsection should also set out any disapplications of the provisions of the National Curriculum in terms of attainment targets, programmes of study and assessment arrangements.

The distinction between educational and non-educational needs and provision

The Code of Practice makes a distinction between educational and non-educational needs and provision. Non-educational needs and provision are meant to be specified at the end of the Statement in Parts 5 and 6. This is confusing when dealing with children with physical difficulties as non-educational needs are not defined, and therefore it is unclear what would constitute non-educational provision.

The Code of Practice makes it quite clear that the NHS is responsible for delivery of the therapy services whether they are specified in Part 3 as education provision or in Part 6 as non-educational provision. It also states that the objectives for the Provision and the arrangements that have been made for providing for it are detailed. In other words phrases such as 'The child should receive appropriate physiotherapy' are not adequate.

Given the holistic and collaborative approach that has been taken to identifying and providing for the child's needs, it is appropriate to integrate all the Provision into Part 3 of the Statement. The child's physical, communication and independent living needs should be specified in Part 2 and the Provision to meet those needs, whether educational or non-educational, should be specified in Part 3.

This is logical since:

- the Provision to meet these needs is usually provided during the school day;
- part of the Provision is provided by educational personnel (e.g. TAs); and
- the Provision should be integral to the National Curriculum, for example the curriculum for Physical Education and English.

However, the responsibility for providing the physiotherapy (or other health services) remains with the NHS even when it has been specified in Part 3. The Code of Practice directs schools, LEAs and the NHS to cooperate closely. The issue for LEAs is ensuring health trusts deliver what they have specified in their Advice, not about taking responsibility for delivering their therapy services.

Clarifying provision

Special provision can be conveniently divided into two areas. The first area is the physical resources:

- school adaptations;
- classroom adaptations;
- equipment; and
- curriculum modifications.

The second area is the personnel resources that are required. These include:

- learning support.
- specialised support (e.g. physiotherapy) in school; and
- teaching adaptations.

Clarifying provision means addressing the issue of how the objectives and targets can be best met. Once again, it is important to recognise that different people will have different views on how each target can be met. This should be seen as one of the benefits of working in a multidisciplinary team, rather than as a difficulty. If the secondary team works together collaboratively they can come up with a range of strategies or programmes to meet the child's targets.

A useful technique to achieve this is called a 'How/How' diagram (Figure 7.3). The target to be achieved is placed in a box on the left of the page. The question 'How?' is then asked. 'How . . . can this be achieved?' The technique means a range of solutions are generated and the team can decide which ones they will use.

Once the 'How/How' is completed, the implications for these in terms of physical and personnel resources can be matched onto the summary tables (Tables 7.1 and 7.2).

Equipment

The provision of equipment is an inter-agency issue. For children with physical disabilities in Britain, equipment for use in school may be purchased by one of three funding agencies – and sometimes by none. For example, health services have some responsibilities for purchasing wheelchairs and communication aids. Their responsibility for wheelchairs overlaps with social services, which also has a responsibility for seating systems. It is not unknown for children only to have an indoor wheelchair and to be expected to purchase their own for outdoor use (going into the playground). The purchase of communication aids is another area of shared responsibility. In this case the overlap is between the LEA and health services. In the past it has not been unknown for a child whose communication aid has been purchased by a LEA to be asked to return it when he leaves a school. This should change following the DfES' £10 million initiative in 2001 to provide information and communication technology for schools. The money is to be used for equipment for pupils with communication difficulties across the curriculum. The British Educational Communications and Technology Agency (BECTa) is managing this project, working closely with the ACE centres in Oldham and

Physical Resources

Physical difficulty	Objective	Target	School adaptation	Classroom adaptation	Equipment	Curriculum modification
Mobility						
Head control						
Sitting						
Using hands						

Visual difficulties	Objective	Target	School adaptation	Classroom adaptation	Equipment	Curriculum modification
Visual input						
Visual processing						

Auditory difficulties	Objective	Target	School adaptation	Classroom adaptation	Equipment	Curriculum modification
Conductive						
Sensorineural						

Medical difficulties	Objective	Target	School adaptation	Classroom adaptation	Equipment	Curriculum modification
Epilepsy						
Other (specify)						

Independent living	Objective	Target	School adaptation	Classroom adaptation	Equipment	Curriculum modification
Dressing						
Undressing						
Mealtimes						
Toileting						

Communication skills	Objective	Target	School adaptation	Classroom adaptation	Equipment	Curriculum modification
Interactional skills						
Speech						
Comprehension						

Learning difficulties	Objective	Target	School adaptation	Classroom adaptation	Equipment	Curriculum modification
In all subjects						
Reading						
Mathematics						
Writing						

Social, emotional or behavioural difficulties	Objective	Target	School adaptation	Classroom adaptation	Equipment	Curriculum modification
Relationship with adults						
Relationship with peers						
Self-esteem						

Table 7.2   Physical resources – summary table

Oxford. This initiative should help ensure that equipment to assist communication should be readily available.

Any equipment that is required to meet needs should be specified in the Statement. It should also be clear who will be purchasing it. Sometimes joint funding is specified and this can be entirely appropriate.

Personnel resources

In addition to the physical resources, a key aspect of the provision is personnel or teaching resources. Teaching is used here in the broadest sense of the word to include all adults who are involved in helping to maintain and develop the child's skills. So teaching resources is used here to include the TA, physiotherapist, speech

Professional	Direct work	Monitoring	Consultancy
TA	Physical support for Jim within classroom every 30 minutes to help reposition. Twenty minutes of individual work with Jim every morning to undertake physical management programme.	Liaison with physiotherapy weekly. Attendance at termly secondary team meeting.	Advice to teacher
Physiotherapist	Weekly work on programme of physical management to improve and maintain muscle strength for repositioning.	Termly meeting with secondary team to review progress.	
Occupational therapist			Termly meeting with secondary team to review progress.

Table 7.3 Example of objective: to be able to position himself independently

Personnel Resources

Professional	Objective	Direct work	Monitoring	Consultancy
Teacher				
Teaching assistant				
Physiotherapist				
Occupational therapist				
Speech and language therapist				
Psychologist				
Other				

Table 7.4 Personnel resources – summary table

and language therapist and anyone else who will be involved in meeting the child's needs. In Chapter 4, three levels of work were described: direct work; monitoring; and consultancy. Depending on the degree of difficulty that the child has he may need help at all these levels.

Each objective needs to be examined in turn to see who will be involved in ensuring it is reached. For example, if the objective is for the child to be able to position himself independently, a number of professionals may be involved (Table 7.3).

Once the personnel provision required for each objective is completed then the information can be transferred to a summary table (Table 7.4). This then gives an overall picture of the personnel resources required.

Monitoring the child's progress

The third aspect of provision specifies the arrangements for setting the short-term targets and how these will be reviewed. This should be done at the Annual Review which is arranged by the school. For children under 5 it is recommended by the Revised Code of Practice that there should also be an informal review of the Statement every six months. The child's progress, as monitored at the Annual Review, should lead directly to the termly meetings to review the Individual Educational Plan.

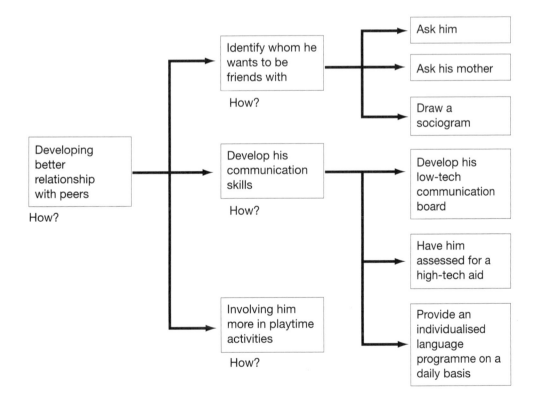

Figure 7.3   'How/How' diagram

School placement

Section 4 of the Statement names the school or nursery the child should attend. The school named must be able to provide the special help set out in Part 3 of the Statement. Before the Statement is finalised a Proposed Statement will be sent to the parents with Section 4 left blank. Parents will be asked to state their preference for which state school they want their child to attend. The LEA must agree with the parents' choice of school as long as:

- the school they choose is suitable for the child's age, ability and special educational needs;
- the child's presence there will not affect the efficient education of the other children already in the school; and
- placing the child in the school will be an efficient use of the LEA's resources.

If the child does not have a completed Statement his teacher should be aware if the parents are going to support placement in the school. The staff should find out during the assessment period if the parents are unhappy and should try to ascertain what their concerns are. These can then be addressed before the Proposed Statement is issued. The parents should be happy about the placement decision.

In a similar way the school should also be happy about the Proposed Statement. Are all the needs identified and also the provision to meet those needs? If not, now is the time to discuss these with the LEA.

If the school or the parents are not happy with the placement, they need to be clear about what their objections are. This needs to be thought about in terms of which of the child's Needs the school cannot meet and/or what, in terms of Provision, the school cannot provide.

Summary

If the Statement is inadequate then the teacher needs to advocate to have it changed. This is done to protect the child and to establish his rights. This chapter has provided the basis for understanding the Statement so that the teacher is in a position to advocate for the child's rights. To do this effectively the teacher should keep the following points in mind.

- **Knowledge-based:**
  - **know the facts:** have a good understanding of the Needs of the child (including the child's view);
  - **know the procedures:** have a good understanding of the Code of Practice.

- Good records:
  - **get things in writing**: make sure that the Statement is accurately written;
  - **draw attention to discrepancies**: compare the written Statement to what is happening in practice;
  - **keep written records**: keep a log of missed visits, direct work, monitoring, and consultations;
  - **put things in writing**: send written requests (for advice, equipment etc.). Make certain you date requests and keep a record.
- Reviews:
  - **monitor progress**: keep accurate record of the child's targets and IEPs and whether they have been achieved;
  - **use opportunities in a positive way**: use reviews as an opportunity to improve things for the child;
  - **organisational not individual**: recognise problem is not simply about the individual child but an organisational issue.
- Personnel:
  - **work collaboratively**: don't become isolated – work collaboratively with a team of people including the parents;
  - **separate the people from the problem**: don't see the other people as the problem; be hard on the problem, not on the people;
  - **don't be personal**: you are acting as the child's teacher to support them (in the same way any teacher would);
  - **don't become emotional**: stay cool but recognise the emotional aspects – 'This is a pretty difficult Review.'

Inclusion is not ultimately about the individual child and his Statement; it is about values, cooperation and resources. It is important, therefore, to see the child's problems within the school context and as part of the wider system. This is what is dealt with in the final chapter.

CHAPTER 8

Changing Together

The effective inclusion of children is a dynamic process. Schools can be seen to go through a journey towards inclusion (Salisbury *et al.* 1993). Not only do the children with physical difficulties grow and change, but so also do the adults around them – teachers, parents and the school as an organisation. Transition points become particularly important. These may include simply a change of teacher but also more major changes such as the transition from nursery to infant school or from junior to secondary school. Such transition points create opportunities for adults to take on new roles. So a teacher can change from being a champion for the child to that of mentor. Or they can change from resignation mode to that of normalisation. At the same time legislative changes also give the opportunity to move towards more inclusive schools.

Special Educational Needs and Disability Act

In September 2002 the Special Educational Needs and Disability Act (SENDA) came into force. It amended the Disability Discrimination Act 1995, which had exempted education from the Act. From September 2002 it became unlawful to discriminate against any disabled child – including those with a physical disability.

It is not the individual teacher's responsibility to ensure that there is no discrimination against the disabled child. Instead, within a maintained school it is the governing body that is responsible for ensuring that disabled children are not discriminated against. In nursery schools it is the LEA.

What is meant by discrimination is 'less favourable treatment'. In other words, a child with a physical disability cannot have less favourable treatment than his peers. In addition, the school has to make reasonable adjustments to ensure that pupils with disabilities are not placed at a substantial disadvantage.

The Act covers three key areas:

- Admissions
- Exclusion
- Education and associated services.

Admissions

A school cannot simply refuse to accept an application from a child who has a physical disability. This is unlawful. As discussed in detail in Chapter 7, a school is expected to meet the child's SEN by providing the provision outlined in the Statement. If it is unable to do so (with the support from the LEA), then it may reasonably argue that admitting the child would be unethical. However, this would have to be a logical, well-argued position, probably supported by the parents. The days when a head teacher or governing body simply said 'We don't take children in wheelchairs' are in the past.

Exclusions

In the same way, a school cannot discriminate against a disabled child by excluding him because of his disability. This is less likely to occur than being refused admission. However, children in wheelchairs or with epilepsy can be seen as a potential danger and it has not been unknown for such children to be excluded on this basis. This is now unlawful.

Education and associated services

This is a broad term that covers many aspects of school life. For example, it covers:

- the curriculum
- teaching and learning
- classroom organisation
- timetabling
- grouping of pupils
- breaks and lunchtimes
- the serving of school meals
- interaction with peers
- school trips
- access to school facilities.

Many of these have been covered in detail throughout this book. For example, ensuring access to school facilities means that it would now be unlawful to exclude children with physical difficulties from certain areas of the school, for example the library or certain classrooms. Schools have until September 2005 to ensure that physical changes in terms of access are made.

As the Special Educational Needs and Disability Act is relatively new, it is important to consider the implications for school policy and practice. The issues are illustrated with some case studies adapted from the SENDA Code of Practice.

Example 1: Admissions

A five-year-old child with a physical difficulty is unable to control his bowel or bladder.

Reaction One: his local mainstream school says it is unable to accept him as it is school policy that children have to be toilet-trained before they start.

Comment: this is discriminatory policy as it means children with a physical difficulty and toileting problems could not be admitted. The school will need to change its policy.

Reaction Two: his local mainstream school says that they are unable to accept him because they do not have appropriate toileting facilities in place.

Comment: this is discriminatory as it means that the school has not been adapted for children with toileting difficulties. The school, in conjunction with the LEA, need to build such facilities immediately.

Reaction Three: his local mainstream school says that they are unable to accept him because they do not have the expertise to teach him toilet-training skills.

Comment: If toileting skills are part of his Special Educational Needs, as specified on the Statement, then the LEA must provide the resources, in terms of expertise, to ensure that he can be taught toileting skills. However, toileting skills may not be part of his SEN, in which case it is an issue to be managed, rather than a focus for development.

Example 2: Exclusions

A seven-year-old boy with mild hemiplegia is subject to temper tantrums.

Reaction One: his local mainstream school excludes him as he is unable to control his temper.

Comment: this is probably discriminatory against the child, as it is known that many children with hemiplegia have difficulties controlling their temper.

Reaction Two: his local mainstream school excludes him because he is a risk to the safety of other pupils.

Comment: Whether this is discriminatory probably depends on whether the school has been able to make reasonable adjustments to the child's education. If they have, with LEA involvement, provided direct and indirect support for the child it may not be discriminatory. The more appropriate path to exclusion would be to review the child's Statement to see if his needs (emotional and behavioural) could be met in the present placement.

Example 3: Educational and associated services

An eight-year-old boy with severe spastic quadriplegia and no speech attends his local mainstream school.

Reaction One: his local mainstream school wants him to spend his mornings in a separate classroom with a TA as his vocalisation disturbs the other pupils.

Comment: This boy would be receiving less favourable treatment than his peers. The reason for being separated is because of his disability. Therefore, this practice is discriminatory and unlawful.

Reaction Two: his school want him to spend his afternoons with a TA in a separate classroom in order to be taught a specific AAC strategy.

Comment: This boy is now receiving different, but maybe not less favourable, treatment to his peers. The school, through its specialist support and its speech and language therapist, would need to make a convincing argument that such an arrangement was in the boy's interest. In this case it would not be discriminatory.

Reaction Three: the school does not want to take him on field trips as they feel the effort involved would outweigh any benefit he might have.

Comment: The school would be discriminating against the boy by not allowing him to go on any field trips. This would be unlawful. However, there might be particular field trips where the boy's safety would be put at risk. If, following a risk assessment by the school, it felt it had reasonable grounds for not allowing the boy to go, this would be lawful.

Over the next few years the SENDA will change the way schools respond to children with disabilities. The above examples illustrate how important it is not to discriminate by treating a child with a disability less favourably than his peers. The duty of the school is to make reasonable adjustments in relation to admissions, exclusions and educational arrangements so that the child with a physical disability is not placed at a substantial disadvantage. Much of the thinking for this about an individual child will take place within the framework of the Code of Practice. However, SENDA also provides the opportunity for work to be undertaken at a whole-school level to develop present policies and practice to ensure effective inclusion. In order to achieve this, the school has a duty to prepare an Accessibility Plan as detailed by the DfES (2001b). Nurseries also require an Accessibility Plan but the responsibility for this remains with the LEA.

The Accessibility Plan

Schools had to prepare an initial Accessibility Plan by April 2003. The plan has three strands:

- to increase access to the schools' curriculum for pupils with a disability;
- to increase access to all areas of the school by improving the physical environment; and
- to improve the written information for children with a disability that is already given to their peers.

The school's accessibility plan should be developed in conjunction with the LEA which also has a duty to write an accessibility strategy for the whole LEA. The LEA's accessibility strategy should inform the school's accessibility plan and vice versa. One process which can help with the development of the accessibility plan is that of MAPS.

MAPS within organisations

In Chapter 3 MAPS was introduced as part of a planning process to help individual planning. However, it can also be used to help school development towards inclusion (York and Tundidor 1995). By mirroring the process of planning for the individual child the school as an organisation can experience some of the issues that surround any development and change.

Membership is a key issue when setting up the MAPS group to work on the accessibility plan. The size of the school as well as the development of other planning will influence who should be involved. It is likely that the head teacher will lead it. The SENCO has a major contribution, as well as other senior teachers responsible for the curriculum and a governor with responsibility for SEN. In addition, a parent of a pupil with a disability and representatives from local disability organisations could make significant contributions. Involvement of other specialists from outside the school should also be considered – an OT with specialist expertise in this area, or the advisory teacher for children with physical disabilities or for sensory impairment. Given the philosophy of MAPS, consideration should also be given to involving pupils. Once again, the involvement of pupils in the process will highlight different ways of looking at many of the issues.

The MAPS process can be seen as three stages with the questions that were used for individual planning adapted for use in the school. The three stages are:

- the present situation
- the preferred situation
- action.

This process takes a broader focus than that required for developing an accessibility plan. However, this helps ensure that the accessibility plan is rooted in the reality of the school development rather than simply another document waiting to be filed.

As with all planning the process is seen as cyclical. The school, having decided on its course of action, needs to review how far it has moved forward before setting new goals and targets.

1. The present situation

Question 1: What is the school's story?
- What is the history of inclusion at this school?
- What are the critical incidents in the past?
- What is the current situation?

One way of helping this process is to draw a picture, or a number of pictures, of the school's story. This can be done as a storyboard showing how the school has reached its present position. It can also be done as one large picture. This rich picture tries to capture in cartoon form how the school is at this moment (Checkland and Scholes 1990).

Question 2: What is the school?
- Think of one word that describes inclusion in the school at this moment.

Question 3: What are the school's strengths, gifts and talents?
- What makes inclusion work in this school?
- Who gives it support and strength?

One thing that may come out of the first part of the process is how little is actually known about some basic issues. For example, does a junior school know how many children between the ages of 3 and 7 with a physical disability are in their catchment area? Does the school have a record of the hours in learning support time that has been available over the last three years? Does anyone have a record of the SEN courses that staff members have attended recently? Before proceeding to the second stage of the process it is often necessary to collect this type of basic information. It is often surprising what is uncovered when such information is collated.

2. *The preferred situation*

The second stage of the process is about developing a vision for the school in terms of inclusion. This means that the school must have a vision for how inclusion will work within the school. This is not the plan for achieving the vision but a picture of what the school would look like if inclusion were to be achieved. This vision then guides the actual planning and decision-making about how to move ahead.

Tied to this vision there needs to be some explicit values. These can be the sort that were explored in Chapter 1. They are about beliefs about inclusion. Values that this book champions are:

- **Rights**: It is only right and proper for children with physical disabilities to be included in mainstream schools.
- **Benefits**: Children with physical disabilities benefit academically and socially from attending mainstream schools.
- **Skills**: Teachers do have the knowledge and skills for successful inclusion.
- **Acceptance**: The inclusion of a child with a physical disability will have a positive effect on his peers.
- **Resources**: Additional resources or support are required for the successful inclusion of children with physical disabilities.

The group needs to discuss what values underpin its vision for inclusion. One of the values that underpins this vision-building is that of diversity. Chapter 2 stresses that every pupil with a physical disability is unique and requires an individual physical management programme. In the same way Chapter 3 examines parents' views on their child with a physical difficulty. Each family will have their own particular expectations depending on their culture and beliefs. Each school needs to plan for managing the environment in terms of adaptations to rooms and buildings. However, each building is unique, and therefore the adaptations required will be unique to that particular school.

In the same way the group needs to recognise that there will be a diversity of views about inclusion. The group needs to recognise and respond to that diversity rather than try to pretend that everyone will agree. Not everyone will have the same values, but by agreeing on what is common and how people differ, there is a basis for moving ahead.

Question 4: What is your dream about inclusion in your school?
- How could inclusion be in the school in 10 years?
- How would things be different for pupils?
- How would things be different for teachers?

Question 5: What is your nightmare?
- What is your biggest fear about inclusion?
- How could it go wrong?

The group can now draw a new 'rich picture'. This time the picture is of how the school would be if the vision was operating perfectly. In particular, the group should think through how the three key aspects of the accessibility plan can be incorporated into the picture. That is:

- increasing access to the school's curriculum for pupils with a disability;
- increasing access to all areas of the school by improving the physical environment; and
- improving the written information for children with a disability that is already given to their peers.

3. Action

In the same way that individual plans are set for the child, organisational plans can be developed for the school.

Question 6: What are the school's needs?
- What are the most important things to change to become a more inclusive school?
- What things must be done inside the school?
- What things must be done in the wider community?
- What does the LEA need to do?
- What do the other agencies need to do?

Question 7: What are our goals and targets?
- What clear goals can we set in response to Question 6?
- What would be appropriate yearly targets for each of these goals?

These can be summarised in the accessibility plan that can also draw upon the individual planning for children as outlined in Chapter 7.

Question 8: How can inclusion be evaluated?
The final question is about ensuring a system is in place to evaluate the effectiveness of inclusion. This can be at both the individual and school levels. At the individual level it is about the child developing new skills and progressing on the National Curriculum. This is based on the child's Statement, the monitoring of progress through the Annual Review, setting targets and the IEP. Through this

process it is possible to evaluate the effectiveness of inclusion for the individual child. This information on individual children can then be analysed. In which areas do children seem to make good progress? In which areas are there concerns?

At the school level it is about developing a more inclusive school. This can be monitored partly by seeing if the targets set on the accessibility plan are being achieved. However, this plan only covers some of the areas that may need to be developed. Developing a more inclusive school can be seen in a whole range of changes. For example, it can be seen by

- change in the number of children who use wheelchairs in the school;
- change in the number of TAs employed by the school; and
- changes in the number of classrooms that become fully accessible.

At another level the development of inclusion may also be monitored through changes in teaching practice. For example, it can be seen by

- changes in the need for the child to be taught outside the classroom;
- change in the amount of direct teaching done by the class teacher;
- changes in the groupings of students to foster cooperative learning; and
- changes in the flexibility of teachers and TAs in their roles.

Targets in some of these areas can be added to the accessibility plan (Table 8.1). This will provide a more holistic view on the changes the school needs to make.

Promoting change

So far, the development of a more inclusive school for children with physical difficulties has been presented as a logical three-step process: present situation; preferred situation; and action. In reality, change in schools is much more complex and often relies on individual members of staff providing the energy and drive to make change happen. Planning to make schools more inclusive can often be stressful as it involves conflict.

In the same way as it is stressful to champion for the individual child, it is also stressful and emotional to champion for a change to a more inclusive school. Change usually involves conflict with people who do not wish to change. This conflict can simply be a lack of cooperation, but there can also be deliberate obstruction and even isolation for one who champions inclusion. There are a number of issues that can underpin this conflict:

Values: Teachers in a school, as well as parents and professionals, will have a range of views on most subjects – and certainly one as contentious as inclusion. It is helpful to recognise that conflict is inevitable given that individuals have a right to have a different view. Chapter 1 explored some of the issues to

Improving the physical environment of the school	Goals	Target (Date)	Target (Date)	Target (Date)	Target (Date)	Target (Date)
School adaptation						
Classroom adaptation						
Equipment						
Other						
Increasing access to the school's curriculum						
Teacher and LSA information and training						
Curriculum development						
Classroom organisation and support						
Timetabling and curriculum options						
Other						
Improvement of written information						
Alternative formats, e.g. Braille, audio tapes						
Oral information, e.g. sign language, symbol system						
Other						

Table 8.1   Accessibility plan

do with inclusion, and though it is helpful to be aware of the research, this knowledge will not in itself change a person's deeply held beliefs.

Needs/interests: Conflict can be about different people's interests. So a head teacher may want resources to be put into a particular area while a class teacher feels that these resources could be better directed elsewhere. A teacher may feel that the child should be withdrawn for language work, while the SENCO wants the speech therapist to be used in the classroom.

Communication: Conflict is often about a failure of communication. Sometimes this is a genuine misunderstanding, where information has not been passed on to a teacher or other member of staff. Sometimes, unfortunately, it can also be done deliberately – such as withholding of budget information about a child's entitlement to support or equipment.

Though conflict is stressful it can also be constructive. Many of the most important changes in our society have come about through conflict. Most of the leaders who have shaped the modern world have recognised that conflict is inevitable to achieve change: Mahatma Gandhi, Nelson Mandela, Martin Luther King. Recognising that conflict is constructive is important, as it gives emotional strength to championing change.

Strategies for handling conflict

Strategies for handling conflict can be described along two dimensions:

- **Assertiveness** – the extent to which the teacher satisfies her own concerns or interests;
- **Cooperativeness** – the extent to which the teacher tries to satisfy others' concerns or interests.

This leads to four main ways of handling conflict (see Figure 8.1):

- advocate;
- negotiate;
- accommodate;
- abdicate.

Advocate

Chapter 7 looks at how advocacy should be the initial strategy of choice if there is conflict over the child's Statement. This is because there are clear guidelines about the procedures for statementing and what a Statement should look like. If these are not being followed then the child's rights are being ignored and it is important for someone to advocate on his behalf. Advocacy involves trying to ensure that *your* position is chosen rather than the other person's. This is known as a 'Win/Lose' – you win, they lose. It is important to advocate when there is a right at stake. Advocacy is not simply used for protecting the rights of children with a physical disability; it can also be used to support the rights of parents or the TA. At another level, the head teacher will be advocating for the rights of the school with the LEA and other agencies such as health trusts and social services.

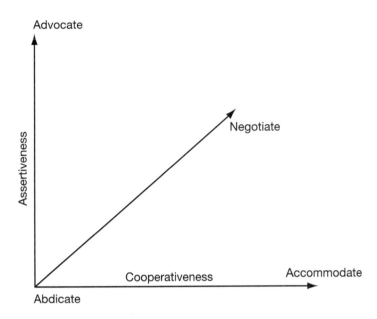

Figure 8.1   Strategies for handling conflict

Accommodate

Accommodating is giving way from a position. This is seen as a 'Lose/Win'. Accommodating is very important when working with other people on complex problems. One of the benefits of accommodating is that it builds trust and encourages a positive relationship between people. It reduces conflict, and is seen as helpful, supportive and encouraging. It leads to goodwill and fosters cooperative relationships. Sometimes it will be really important to accommodate to move forward the agenda for inclusion in a school. For example, a conflict might arise about where the physiotherapist could work in school. Though it might not be convenient for the teachers, agreeing that the physiotherapist can use the school hall may be a way of resolving a particular conflict. Such a resolution is likely to build trust and flexibility between people and lead to a better resolution of other conflicts in the future.

Abdicate

Abdication avoids moving forward or solving a problem. Abdication is often unhelpfully used when there is conflict. The problem is that nothing is resolved and the problem is likely to reoccur sooner or later.

Negotiate

Negotiation involves trying to find a solution to a conflict with which both sides are happy. This is described as a 'Win/Win'. Negotiation recognises that when moving towards a more inclusive school there is considerable ambiguity. There is often not one simple way of doing things. Instead, people will have different points of view about what the priorities are and how they should be tackled. So, for example, it may be entirely appropriate to advocate for the need for the school to become more inclusive. This can be seen as a right or a principle. However, how the school is to become more inclusive is something that will need to be negotiated between people – teachers, parents and children. The purpose of negotiation is to represent oneself fairly so that a wise outcome is reached efficiently. This should be the strategy of choice most of the time when trying to achieve a more inclusive school.

In many situations where there is conflict, there is no clear structure for deciding on how to resolve them. This is where negotiation comes in as a way of solving joint problems (Fisher and Ury 1981). Many of the similar principles for advocacy can be used for negotiation. There are two parts to successful negotiation: the preparation and then the actual negotiation.

Preparing for negotiation

The preparation ensures that you know what is likely to come up. Unlike advocacy you need to think about how the other person sees the issues.

Issues: Identify your problem but also the problem faced by the other. By identifying their problem it gives you a good indication of their motivation.

Facts and technical details: Identify relevant facts and make certain they are accurate.

Interests – theirs and mine: Identify your, and the other side's, goals, interests and priorities. Identify the strengths and weaknesses of their position.

Multiple solutions – do not get stuck on one solution. Generate a range of possible solutions if you can.

Best possible BATNA: BATNA stands for Best Alternative To a Negotiated Agreement. It is good to identify what you will do if negotiations fail. This can then be used as a reference point to compare any proposal. The better your BATNA the stronger your negotiating position.

The actual negotiation

The preparation for negotiation can be seen as a rehearsal for the actual negotiation. Good negotiation depends on good communication skills, that is establishing a good rapport through listening and empathy.

Common problems: It is helpful to start by agreeing the nature and purpose of the problem. It is important to listen to the other side and confirm that you both think that there is a problem.

Common interests/needs: Move on from the common problem to describe, in general terms, the situation that you would like to see. Let the other person describe how they would ideally see it. Is there common ground that can be reached?

Options for mutual gain: Focus on what you would both get out of the new scenario.

A way forward: Both try to describe how you will do things differently. Try to reach agreement.

Review: It is often helpful to set a review date. This confirms that you are seriously interested in progress. It should be far enough ahead to see if the agreed way forward has yielded any results.

Negotiation will not resolve all problems. The other side may be too powerful and may not want to negotiate. You can really only negotiate if both sides recognise that there is a problem. The first step, therefore, may be establishing that there is a problem. For example, the physiotherapist may wish to carry out the physical management programme on a Wednesday afternoon in the classroom with the TA. This, however, may be a very poor time for you as you are wishing to do Art at that time and there are implications for classroom space. The first thing is to establish that there is a common issue. It is important to try to get the other side to see the merits of resolving the problem. Try to see it from their point of view. Maybe they do not have a problem. It may be helpful to get a third party in to try to help. Negotiation works when there is a mutual problem that two people want to resolve.

Building an inclusive school

Analysis of how schools move towards inclusion demonstrates that individual people are at the heart of the process. Though most of the perceived barriers are resources, it is individual people who make inclusion work. This is why this book stresses the importance of teachers championing for inclusion. Three strategies can be used to gain power and champion effectively:

- build resources
- share information
- create alliances.

Build resources

Building up resources is a source of power. The source of many resources is money. Money can buy time for children with physical difficulties, in terms of TAs, equipment and adaptations to the school. Attracting money to the school is therefore crucial, as is good financial management. However, resources are not simply to do with money. The most important resource for successful inclusion is the people in the school community. Individual teachers' and TAs' expertise and commitment are at the heart of this. The school that can recruit, retain and develop a dynamic staff team has the most important resource for successful inclusion.

Share information

One way of retaining and building resources is to develop information networks. These are networks of key people or organisations who have information that can be valuable to the school. Some of these networks will be formal, for example the link with the LEA to ensure the school's accessibility plan builds on the LEA's Strategic Plan. Some of these networks will be informal, for example knowing of a speech and language therapist who specialises in children's Augmentative and Alternative Communication systems. In addition, information – in terms of local resources provided by voluntary agencies, knowledge of specialist conditions from the internet and links with developments in other schools throughout the country – gives a school an invaluable resource for developing inclusion.

Create alliances

The sharing of information leads to the development of alliances. Alliances are methods of creating influence without any formal authority. A theme which is present throughout the book is that of collaborative teamwork. There are a whole range of people who are keys to the successful education inclusion of children with physical difficulties. Making inclusion work is about power. It is about empowering the child with physical difficulties so that he can have an active life in the classroom, and about empowering peers so that they can contribute to that process. However, it is also about empowering teachers, TAs and other professionals so that they can work as a team to make inclusion happen. In the same way as the team supporting the child can be seen as an alliance, so can the team supporting the development of the school. The alliance can be seen as a group of people without a formal structure, focused on shared goals which require concerted members' actions.

Drawing a sociogram (see Chapter 6) provides a map of how people group around the issue of inclusion in the school. The child's teacher can put herself in the centre of the map. She can then draw her closest allies for inclusion nearest to her. On Figure 8.2 the strength of support for inclusion is indicated by a plus sign and those opposed to inclusion are indicated by a minus sign. The lines between people indicate alliances.

Coalition leaders

Identifying key members of various coalitions helps to narrow the number of people requiring attention. The key member of the coalition acts as a lever by which several people can be influenced. In the example (Figure 8.2) there is a good relationship between the teacher and Mavis and Jane, both of whom are coalition leaders. Mavis is a coalition leader as she influences other parents and the head teacher. Ensuring she uses this influence may move the head teacher's position on inclusion. In the same way Jane, the SENCO, has some influence over the TA and the deputy head. These coalition leaders become an important part of the alliance.

Activity

If most people have only a limited involvement in moving the school to inclusion, the first step is raising the level of activity. Telling people about the need for an accessibility plan should be a priority. If most people are against further inclusion of children with physical difficulties you will need to identify some powerful allies. In Figure 8.2 both the head teacher and deputy head are against further inclusion.

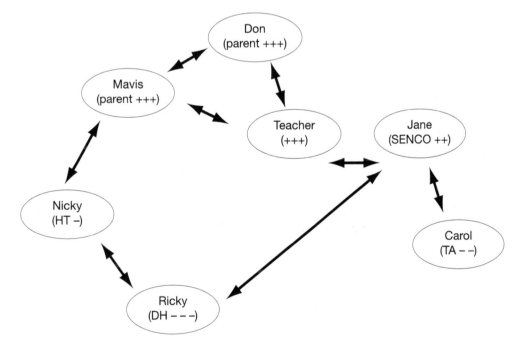

Figure 8.2   Inclusion alliance

You will need to muster the support of the parents and SENCO and maybe look further afield to the LEA for support. If people with power support inclusion but are not very active, the first step is to increase their activity level.

Attention priority

Priority attention should be given to those people who may change their position. This is particularly important if they have a lot of power. In the example the head teacher is only slightly against inclusion (–). It may be that attention should be given to her rather than to the deputy head who seems to be strongly against it (– – –). These people should get attention in terms of promoting the inclusion plan.

It is important to recognise and acknowledge that different people in a school will take different positions on the inclusion of children with physical difficulties – particularly those with severe physical difficulties. Championing effectively does mean creating alliances with others and getting their support to build a more inclusive school.

Getting started

It is often very difficult to know how to get started and from whom to get help. A good starting point is other teachers of children with physical difficulties. These teachers may be in your school or in neighbouring schools. They will be addressing similar issues. Other teachers may have, in the past, successfully included children with physical difficulties in their classrooms. Listen to their stories – who supported them?

In some LEAs there may be support, or work discussion, groups for teachers involved in inclusion of children with physical difficulties. Ask at the local teachers' centre if there is such a group in your area. If there is not, you could consider starting one?

The journey

The inclusion of children with physical difficulties does not have an end point. It is difficult to envisage a time when all children will achieve full inclusion in our schools. This book is about a journey, not about the destination. Not only are there differences in severity of difficulties there are also differences in levels of inclusion. So, initially, it may be difficult to include a child with a wheelchair in a school. However, as the school develops, this no longer becomes a challenge and the next challenge comes into view, for example including a child who uses an AAC system. The next year there may be a child with an AAC system but who also has learning difficulties. The point is that each child presents fresh challenges that need to be planned for.

If the school has good resources, good information and strong alliances, the only question left is making it work. However, for many schools and teachers the arrival of a child with a physical disability is just the beginning of a long and challenging journey. The teacher (and TA, head teacher and all the other staff) may have to learn to champion for the child, to negotiate on his behalf and to mentor and support other members of staff. The endpoint of this is a normalisation of inclusion for children with physical disabilities.

This is difficult when all you really want to be is a good class teacher for all pupils. This journey, of including all children with physical disabilities, is not easy. It is important, therefore, to be able to advocate your position about mainstream education in a way that gains you allies.

However, many teachers in the long run find the journey empowering. You learn more about how to manage the classroom in innovative ways, how to work with other people and to team-teach. You learn how to negotiate, to advocate and to plan. You learn to work with other agencies and professionals with different skills and backgrounds. Most importantly, you learn that children with physical disabilities are, in the final analysis, simply children who need some of the power that teachers hold in their heads, hands and hearts. It is by using this power that teachers can make inclusion for children with physical difficulties a reality.

References

Ainscow, M. (1999) *Understanding the Development of Inclusive Schools*. London: Falmer.

Ainscow, M. and Sebba, J. (eds) (1996) 'International developments in inclusive education'. *Cambridge Journal of Education* (Special issue), **26**, 1.

Anderson, E. (1973) *The Disabled Schoolchild: A Study of Integration in Primary Schools*. London: Methuen.

Anderson, E. (1975) 'A research study on the integration of physically handicapped children in ordinary primary schools', in Loring, J. and Burn, G., *Integration of Handicapped Children in Society*. London: Routledge and Kegan Paul.

Appleton P., Minchen, P., Ellis, N. *et al.* (1994) 'The self-concept of young people with spina bifida: a population-based study'. *Developmental Medicine and Child Neurology*, **36**, 198–215.

Audit Commission (2002) *Statutory Assessments and Statements of Special Educational Needs: In Need of Review?* London: Audit Commission

Bailey, D. (1987) 'Collaborative goal-setting with families: resolving differences in values and priorities for services'. *Topics in Early Childhood Special Education*, 7(2), 59–71

Bailey, D. and Winton, P. (1987) 'Stability and change in parents' expectations about mainstreaming'. *Topics in Early Childhood Special Education*, 7(1), 73–87.

Bairstow, P., Cochrane, R. and Hur, J. (1993) *Evaluation of Conductive Education for Children with Cerebral Palsy. Final Report Parts 1 and 2*. London: HMSO.

Baker, E. (1994) 'Meta-analytic evidence for non-inclusive educational practice: does educational research support current practice for special needs students?' Doctoral Dissertation, Temple University, Philadelphia.

Baker, E., Wang, M. and Walberg, H. (1995) 'The effect of inclusion on learning'. *Educational Leadership*, **52**(4), 33–5.

Barton, M. (1992) *Teachers' Opinions on the Implementation and Effects of Mainstreaming*. Chicago: Chicago Public schools.

Bennett, T., Deluca, D. and Bruns, D. (1997) 'Putting inclusion into practice: perspectives of teachers and parents'. *Exceptional Children*, **64** (1), 115–31.

Beresford, B. (1995) *Expert Opinions: A National Survey of Parents Caring for a Severely Disabled Child.* York: Joseph Rowntree Foundation.

Berryman, J. and Berryman, C. (1981) 'Use of the "Attitudes Toward Mainstreaming Scale" with rural Georgia teachers'. Paper presented at an American Educational Research Association meeting, Los Angeles (ERIC Document Reproduction Service No. ED 201 420).

Booth, T. (1981) 'Demystifying integration', in Swann, W., *The Practice of Special Education.* Oxford: Basil Blackwell.

Booth, T., Ainscow, M. and Dyson, A. (1997) 'Understanding inclusion and exclusion in the English competitive education system'. *International Journal of Inclusive Education,* 1(4), 337–55.

Bower, E. and McLellan, D. (1994) 'Measuring motor goals in children with CP'. *Clinical Rehabilitation,* 8, 198–206.

Bowley, A. (1969) 'A follow-up of 64 children with cerebral palsy'. *Developmental Medicine and Child Neurology,* 9(2), 172–82.

British Picture Vocabulary Test (BPVT). Windsor: NFER-Nelson.

Byrne, E. and Cunningham, C. (1985) 'The effects of mentally handicapped children on families: a conceptual review'. *Journal of Child Psychology and Psychiatry,* 26, 847–64.

CALL (Communication Aids for Language and Learning) (1997) *Person Passports.* Edinburgh: CALL.

Carlberg, C. and Kavale, K. (1980) 'The efficacy of special versus regular class placement for exceptional children: a meta-analysis'. *Journal of Special Education,* 14, 295–309.

Center, Y. and Ward, J. (1984) 'Integration of mildly handicapped cerebral palsied children into regular schools'. *The Exceptional Child,* 31(2), 104–13.

Center, Y., Ward, J. and Ferguson, C. (1991) 'Towards an index to evaluate the integration of children with disabilities into regular classes'. *Educational Psychology,* 11(1), 77–95.

Champeau, T. (1992) 'Transactional analysis and rehabilitation: an integrative approach to disability'. *Transactional Analysis Journal,* 22(4), 234–42.

Checkland, P. and Scholes, J. (1990) *Soft System Methodology in Action.* Chichester: Wiley.

Cioni, G., Paolicelli, P., Sordi, C. and Vinter, A. (1993) 'Sensorimotor development in cerebral-palsied infants assessed with the Uzgiris-Hunt scales'. *Developmental Medicine and Child Neurology,* 35, 1055–66.

Clark, G. and Seifer, R. (1983) 'Facilitating mother–infant communication'. *Infant Mental Health Journal,* 4, 67–81.

Crocker, J. and Major, B. (1989) 'Social stigma and self-esteem: the self-protective properties of stigma'. *Psychological Review,* 96(4), 608–30.

Darling, R. (1993) 'Parent–professional interaction: the roots of misunderstanding', in Seligman, M. (ed.) *The Family with a Handicapped Child: Understanding and Treatment.* London: Allyn and Bacon.

Deno, E. (1970) 'Special education as development capital'. *Exceptional Children,* 37(3), 229–37.

DES (1989) *Educating Physically Disabled Children.* London: HMSO.

DfEE (1996) *Supporting Pupils with Medical Needs in School* (Circular 14/96). London: HMSO.

DfEE (1997) *Excellence for All Children: Meeting Special Educational Needs.* London: HMSO.

DfEE (1998) *Meeting Special Educational Needs: A Programme for Action.* London: HMSO.

DfES (2001a) *Special Educational Needs Code of Practice.* London: HMSO.

DfES (2001b) *Special Educational Needs and Disability Act.* London: HMSO.

DfES (2001c) *Statistics of Education: Special Educational Needs in England, January 2001.* London: HMSO.

Diamond, K. (1993) 'Preschool children's concept of disability in their peers', *Early Education and Development,* 4, 123–9.

Dutton, G., Day, R. and McCulloch, D. (1999) 'Who is a visually impaired child?' *Developmental Medicine and Child Neurology,* 41, 211–13.

Egan, G. (1990) *The Skilled Helper* (4th edn). Monterey, CA: Brooks-Cole.

Erwin, E. and Soodak, L. (1995) 'I never knew I could stand up to the system: families' perspectives on pursuing inclusive education'. *Journal of The Association for Persons with Severe Handicaps,* 20(2), 136–46.

Evans, P., Johnson, A., Mutch, L. and Alberman, E. (1989) 'A standard form for recording clinical findings in children with a motor deficit of central origin'. *Developmental Medicine and Child Neurology,* 31, 119–27.

Farrell, P. (1997) 'The integration of children with severe learning difficulties: a review of the recent literature'. *Journal of Applied Research in Intellectual Disabilities,* 10(1), 1–14.

Fisher, R. and Ury, W. (1981) *Getting to Yes – Negotiating Agreements Without Giving In.* London: Hutchinson.

Forest, M. and Lusthaus, E. (1990) 'Everyone belongs with the MAPS Action Planning System'. *Teaching Exceptional Children,* 22, 32–5.

Fox, M. (1998) 'Multidisciplinary assessment of under-fives with cerebral palsy', in Wolfendale, S. (ed.) *Meeting Special Needs in the Early Years.* London: David Fulton.

Fox, M. (1999) 'Parents' concerns about the inclusion of children with physical disabilities into mainstream schools'. Unpublished doctoral thesis, University of East London.

Fuchs, D. and Fuchs, L. (1995) 'Sometimes separate is better'. *Educational Leadership,* 52(4), 22–6.

Garvar-Pinhas, A. and Schmelkin, L. (1989) 'Administrators' and teachers' attitudes to mainstreaming'. *Remedial and Special Education*, **10**(4), 38–43.

Giangreco, M. (1997) 'Key lessons learned about inclusive education: summary of the 1996 Schonell Memorial Lecture'. *International Journal of Disability, Development and Education*, **44**(3), 193–206.

Goodman, R. (1997) 'Psychological aspects of hemiplegia'. *Archive Disability in Children*, **76**, 177–8.

Hall, D. and Hill, P. (1996) *The Child with a Disability*. Oxford: Blackwell.

Harter S. (1988) 'Causes, correlates and the functional role of global self-worth: a life-span perspective', in Kolligian, J. and Sternberg, R. (eds) *Perceptions of Competence and Incompetence across the Life-Span*. New Haven, CT: Yale University Press.

Jarrett, N. (1996) 'Inclusive education: theory into practice'. *Educational and Child Psychology*, **13**(3), 76–85.

Jenkinson, J. (1997) *Mainstream or Special: Educating Students with Disabilities*. London: Routledge.

Jenkinson, J. (1998) 'Parent choice in the education of students with disabilities'. *International Journal of Disability, Development and Education*, **45**(2), 189–202.

Johnson, D. and Johnson, F. (1987) *Joining Together: Group Theory and Group Skills*. London: Prentice-Hall.

Kopp, C. and Shaperman, J. (1973) 'Cognitive development in the absence of object manipulation during infancy'. *Developmental Psychology*, **9**(3), 430.

Larrivee, B. (1985) *Effective Teaching for Successful Mainstreaming*, London: Longman.

Levitt, S. (1982) *Treatment of Cerebral Palsy and Motor Delay*. Oxford: Blackwell Scientific Publications.

Lipsky, D. and Gartner, A. (1996) 'Inclusion, school restructuring, and the remaking of American society'. *Harvard Educational Review*, **66**(4), 762–9.

Lodge, J. (1999) 'Developing curriculum access based on sensory approaches: partial sight and blindlness', in Blamires, M. (ed.) *Enabling Technology for Inclusion*. London: Paul Chapman, pp. 83–95.

Logan, K. and Malone, M. (1998) 'Comparing instructional contexts of students with and without severe disabilities in general education classrooms'. *Exceptional Children*, **64**(3), 343–58.

Lovell, C. (2001) *Advocacy*. Course materials, University of Essex.

Lynch, J. (1987) *Prejudice Reduction and the School*. London: Cassell.

McCollum, J. (1984) 'Social interaction between parents and babies: validation of an intervention procedure'. *Childcare, Health and Development*, **10**, 301–15.

Mahoney, G. (1988) 'Maternal communication with mentally retarded children'. *American Journal of Mental Deficiency*, **92**, 341–8.

Male, D. (1998) 'Special educational needs: statistics and trends'. *Tizard Learning Disability Review*, **3**(3), 40–5.

Mandell, C. and Fiscus, E. (1981) *Understanding Exceptional People*. New York: West Publishers.

Marks, S. (1997) 'Reducing prejudice against children with disabilities in inclusive settings'. *International Journal of Disability, Development and Education*, **44**(2), 117–31.

Marlow, E., Thomas, M. and Innes, A. (1968) 'Spastics in ordinary schools'. *Special Education*, **57**(1), 8–15.

Martin, S., Brady, M. and Williams, R. (1991) 'Effects of toys on the social behaviour of preschool children in integrated and non-integrated groups: investigation of a setting event'. *Journal of Early Intervention*, **15**, 152–61.

Mason, M. (1998) *Forced Apart: The Case for Ending Compulsory Segregation in Education*. London: Alliance for Inclusive Education.

Meyer, L. (2001) 'The impact of inclusion on children's lives: multiple outcomes, and friendship in particular'. *International Journal of Disability, Development and Education*, **48**(1), 9–31.

Molnar, G. (1992) 'The influence of psychosocial factors on personality development and emotional health in children with cerebral palsy and spina bifida', in Heller, B., Flohr, L. and Zegans, L. (eds) *Psychosocial Interventions with Physically Disabled Persons*. London: Jessica Kingsley.

MOVE (1995) *International Brochure*. Bakersfield, CA: Kern County Superintendent of Schools' Office.

Nabors, L., Willoughby, J., Leff, S. and McMenamin, S. (2001) 'Promoting inclusion for young children with special needs on playgrounds'. *Journal of Developmental and Physical Disabilities*, **13**(2), 179–89.

Newell, P. (1985) 'Integration, possibilities, practice and pitfalls'. *Education and Child Psychology*, **2**, 3.

Newson, J. (1979) 'Intentional behaviour in the young infants', in Shaffer, D. and Dunn, J. (eds) *The First Year of Life*. New York: Wiley.

Nind, M. and Hewett, D. (1994) *Access to Communication*. London: David Fulton.

Parish, T., Maker, S., Arheart, K. and Adamchak, P. (1980) 'Normal and exceptional children's attitudes towards themselves and one another'. *The Journal of Psychology*, **104**, 249–53.

Pearpoint, J., Forest, M. and Snow, J. (1992) *The Inclusion Papers*. Toronto: Inclusion Press.

Peck, C., Carlson, P. and Helmstetter, E. (1992) 'Parent and teacher perceptions of outcomes for typically developing children enrolled in integrated early childhood programs: a statewide survey'. *Journal of Early Intervention*, **16**, 53–63.

Phillips, W., Allred, K., Brulle, A. and Shank, K. (1990) 'The regular education initiative'. *Teacher Education and Special Education*, **13**, 182–5.

Piaget, J. (1966) *The Origins of Intelligence in Children*. New York: International Universities Press.

Queensland Spastic Welfare League (1993) *Children with Cerebral Palsy in the Classroom: A Guide for Teachers*. Queensland, Australia.

Quinn, P. (1998) *Understanding Disability: A Life-span Approach*. London: Sage.

Rahamin, L. (1999) 'Scaling physical barriers', in Blamires, M. (ed.) *Enabling Technology for Inclusion*. London: Paul Chapman.

Rekate, H. (1990) *Comprehensive Management of Spina Bifida*. Boca Raton, Florida: CRC.

Resnick, M. and Hutton, L. (1987) 'Resilience among physically disabled adolescents'. *Psychiatric-Annals*, **17**(12), 796–800.

Richardson, S., Hastorf, A. and Dornbusch, S. (1964) 'The effects of physical disability on a child's description of himself'. *Child Development*, **35**, 893–907.

Rogers, C. (1983) *Freedom To Learn for the 80s*. New York: Macmillan.

Rose, R. (2001) 'Primary school teacher perceptions of the conditions required to include pupils with special educational needs'. *Educational Review*, **53**(2), 147–56.

Salisbury, C., Palombaro, M. and Hollowood, T. (1993) 'On the nature and change of an inclusive elementary school'. *Journal of the Association for Persons with Severe Handicaps*, **18**(2), 75–84.

Schein, E. (1988*) Organisational Psychology*. London: Prentice-Hall.

Scope (1994) *Right from the Start*. London: Scope.

Scope (1995) *Bobarth: Scope Therapy Factsheet*. London: Scope.

Scope (1998) *Whose Problem Is It?* London: Scope.

Scope (undated) *The Land of Droog*. London: Scope.

Scruggs, T. and Mastropieri, M. (1996) 'Teacher perceptions of mainstreaming/inclusion, 1958–1995: a research synthesis'. *Exceptional Children*, **63**(1), 59–74.

Seligman, M. and Darling, B. (1989) *Ordinary Families and Special Children: A Systems Approach to Childhood Disability*. London: Guildford Press.

Sideridis, G. and Chandler, J. (1997) 'Assessment of teacher attitudes toward inclusion of students with disabilities: a confirmatory factor analysis'. *Adapted Physical Activity Quarterly*, **14**, 51–64.

Skinner, M. (1996) 'Full inclusion and students with disabilities: one size fits all?' *Reading and Writing Quarterly: Overcoming Learning Difficulties*, **12**, 241–4.

Sloper, P. and Turner, S. (1991) 'Parental and professional views of the needs of families with a child with severe physical disability'. *Counselling Psychology Quarterly*, **4**, 323–30.

Sloper, P. and Turner, S. (1993) 'Risk and resistance factors in the adaptation of parents of children with severe physical disability'. *Journal of Child Psychology and Psychiatry*, **34**(2), 167–88.

Society of Education Officers (1996) *SEN Initiatives: Managing Budgets for Pupils with SEN*. London: Coopers and Lybrand.

Stainback, W. and Stainback, S. (1990) *Support Networks for Inclusive Schools: Interdependent Integrated Education*. Baltimore: Paul H. Brooks.

Staub, D. and Peck, C. (1995) 'What are the outcomes for nondisabled students?' *Educational Leadership*, **52**(4), 36–40.

Staub, D., Schwartz, I., Gallucci, C. and Peck, C. (1994) 'Four portraits of friendship at an inclusive school'. *The Journal of the Association for Persons with Severe Handicaps*.

Stolber, K., Gettinger, M. and Goetz, D. (1998) 'Exploring factors influencing parents' and early childhood practitioners' beliefs about inclusion'. *Early Childhood Research Quarterly*, **13**(1), 107–24.

Strully, J. and Strully, C. (1989) 'Friendships as an educational goal', in Stainback, S., Stainback, W. and Forest, M. (eds) *Educating All Students in the Mainstream of General Education*. Baltimore: Brooks, 59–68.

Swain, J., Finkelstein, V., French, S., and Oliver, M. (1993) *Disabling Barriers: Enabling Environments*. London: Sage.

Thomas, G. (1997) 'Inclusive schools for an inclusive society'. *British Journal of Special Education*, **24**(3), 103–7.

Thomas, G., Walker, D. and Webb, J. (1998) *The Making of the Inclusive School*. London: Routledge.

Vandercook, T., York, J. and Forest, M. (1989) 'MAPS: a strategy for building the vision'. *Journal of the Association for Persons with Severe Handicaps*, **14**, 205–15.

Varni, J., Rubenfeld, L. and Talbot, D. (1989) 'Determinants of self-esteem in children with congenital/acquired limb deficiencies'. *Journal of Developmental and Behavioral Paediatrics*, **10**(1), 13–16.

Vincent, D. and de la Mare, M. (1985) *The New Reading Analysis*. Berkshire: NFER-Nelson.

Wang, M. and Baker, T. (1986) 'Mainstreaming programs: design features and effects'. *Journal of Special Education*, **19**, 503–21.

Warnock, M. (1978) *Special Educational Needs. Report of the Committee of Enquiry into Special Educational Needs*. DES/HMSO.

Whorf, B.L. (1956) *Language, Thought and Reality* (edited with an introduction by J. Carroll). New York: Wiley.

Within Reach (1992) National Union of Teachers/The Spastics Society.

Wittrock, M. (ed.) (1985) *Handbook of Research on Teaching*. New York: Collier MacMillan.

Wolfendale, S. (1992) *Empowering Parents and Teachers*. London: Cassell.

York, J. and Tundidor, M. (1995) 'Issues raised in the name of inclusion: perspectives of educators, parents and students, *Journal of the Association for Persons with Severe Handicaps*, **20**(1), 31–44.

York, J., Vandercook, T., MacDonald, C., Heise-Neff, C. and Caughey, E. (1992) 'Feedback about integrating middle school education students with severe disabilities in general education classes'. *Exceptional Children*, **58**(3), 244–58.

Index

The letters 'f' and 't' after a page number indicate inclusion of a figure and table respectively.